CULTURE SMART!
ARMENIA

Susan Solomon

·K·U·P·E·R·A·R·D·

First published in Great Britain 2010
by Kuperard, an imprint of Bravo Ltd
59 Hutton Grove, London N12 8DS
Tel: +44 (0) 20 8446 2440   Fax: +44 (0) 20 8446 2441
www.culturesmartguides.com
Inquiries: sales@kuperard.co.uk

Culture Smart!® is a registered trademark of Bravo Ltd

Distributed in the United States and Canada
by Random House Distribution Services
1745 Broadway, New York, NY 10019
Tel: +1 (212) 572-2844   Fax: +1 (212) 572-4961
Inquiries: csorders@randomhouse.com

Copyright © 2010 Kuperard

Series Editor Geoffrey Chesler
Design Bobby Birchall

ISBN 978 1 85733 493 7

British Library Cataloguing in Publication Data
A CIP catalogue entry for this book is available from the
British Library

Printed in Malaysia

This book is available for special discounts for bulk purchases
for sales promotions or premiums. Special editions, including
personalized covers, excerpts of existing books, and corporate
imprints, can be created in large quantities for special needs.

For more information in the USA write to Special
Markets/Premium Sales, 1745 Broadway, MD 6–2, New York,
NY 10019, or e-mail specialmarkets@randomhouse.com.

In the United Kingdom contact Kuperard publishers at the
address at the top of this page.

Cover image: Khor Virap Monastery with Mount Ararat in background.
© Claudia Dewald/iStockphoto.com
The photographs on pages 77, 86, 87, 121, and 130 are reproduced by permission
of the author.
Images on pages 43 © Pavel Losevsky/fotolia.com; 45 © Mahesh Patil/fotolia.com;
60 © Anna Telnova/fotolia.com; 93 © Matthew Dixon/iStockphoto.com; and
103 © Anna Bryukhanova/iStockphoto.com.
Images on the following pages reproduced under Creative Commons License Attribution
2.0, 2.5, and 3.0: 13 © Andrew Behesnilian; 23 © Giovanni Dall'Orto;
30 © z@doune; 40, 107, 129, and 146 © Bouarf; 51 and 156 © Vigen Hakhverdyan;
62 © Julia Fraedrich from California; 64 © D-man; 67 © Rita Willaert; 72 © Luciana;
88 © RaffiKojian; 95 © Antonov 14; 106 © Julius Schorzman; 117 © avixyz;
123 © Sven Dirks, Wien; 136 and 137 © Mcschreck; and 164 © Deror Avi

About the Author

SUSAN SOLOMON has led the public relations and marketing programs of several large non-profit organizations. She has taught marketing, public relations, and writing at three Southern California universities, and in 2008 went to Armenia on a Fulbright scholarship to teach graduate-level marketing and public relations in Yerevan. To prepare for the journey she studied Armenian language and culture. Her family went with her, and her two children went to school in Yerevan.

Susan has written extensively in her field, and in 2005 published *Building Powerful Health Care Brands*. She has also written travel articles for the *Los Angeles Times* and is currently writing a novel.

The Culture Smart! series is continuing to expand.
For further information and latest titles visit
www.culturesmartguides.com

The publishers would like to thank **CultureSmart!**Consulting for its help in researching and developing the concept for this series.

CultureSmart!Consulting creates tailor-made seminars and consultancy programs to meet a wide range of corporate, public-sector, and individual needs. Whether delivering courses on multicultural team building in the USA, preparing Chinese engineers for a posting in Europe, training call-center staff in India, or raising the awareness of police forces to the needs of diverse ethnic communities, it provides essential, practical, and powerful skills worldwide to an increasingly international workforce.

For details, visit www.culturesmartconsulting.com

CultureSmart!Consulting and **CultureSmart!** guides have both contributed to and featured regularly in the weekly travel program "Fast Track" on BBC World TV.

contents

contents

Map of Armenia

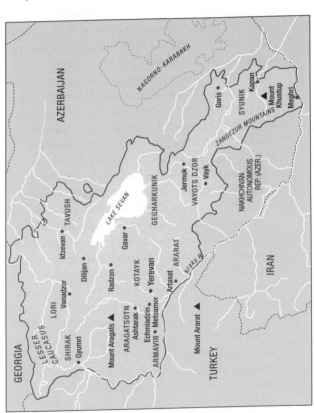

introduction

On a map of the world today, the country of Armenia looks very small. It is about the size of Belgium, or the North American state of Maryland. Landlocked and mountainous, it is bordered by much larger neighbors—Turkey, Azerbaijan, Georgia, and Iran.

Comparisons can be deceptive, however. This tiny nation in the Caucasus Mountains looms very large in the hearts of Armenians, both the three million living within the country and the eight million who are part of the world's Armenian Diaspora. For the Armenian people, who have existed for five thousand years, sometimes without a country to call their own, the modern borders are simply artificial lines drawn by larger foreign powers in the early twentieth century. Geography is much less important than what it means to be Armenian—to have created a proud culture, to have passed it down to one's children, and, most importantly, to have survived in tragic circumstances against almost unbelievable odds.

For the traveler to Armenia, some knowledge about the history and culture of the country is essential to appreciating its people. *Culture Smart! Armenia* provides a concise historical survey from ancient to modern times. More importantly, however, it addresses the way in which thousands of years of struggle have created a cultural memory that continues to define the Armenian people today.

The book looks at how its culture and history have influenced so many elements of modern

Armenia, from family life to getting around the bustling streets of Yerevan and engaging in business. Armenians are far from impenetrable, but it is necessary to understand what makes them the way they are. Many of the people you will meet have survived the bitter days of the early 1990s, when war, blockages, shortages, and the aftermath of a terrible earthquake locked the country into desolation, deprivation, and darkness. They have seen and experienced it all.

Today's Armenia, like that of the past, is a place of challenge and triumph. Still emerging from economic hardship, it faces unemployment, environmental concerns, political unrest, closed borders, corruption, a wavering economy, and widespread emigration. Yet there are signs of change and a new era—construction, revival of the arts, and easing of tensions with the Turkish neighbors. You can also see the "new Armenia" by observing everyday life, from the lavish weddings and other celebrations that take place almost daily, to the attitude of its young people, who are determined to work hard, have fun, and contribute to their country.

Culture Smart! Armenia aims to broaden your understanding of a people whose cultural pride, welcoming nature, and enduring will are known far beyond the borders of their homeland. It will help you to avoid misunderstandings and to make your visit a memorable and rewarding experience.

Key Facts

Official Name	Republic of Armenia Hayastan (Armenian name)	Declared independence from Soviet Union on September 21, 1991
Capital City	Yerevan (pop. 1,107,800)	
Other Major Cities	Gyumri, Vanadzor, Echmiadzin	
Area	11,484 square miles (29,743 sq. km). Landlocked in the Lesser Caucasus Mts.	Slightly smaller than the state of Maryland
Borders	Turkey, Azerbaijan, Georgia, and Iran.	Borders with Turkey and Azerbaijan currently closed
Terrain	Mountainous highlands, fast flowing rivers, few forests	Lake Sevan is the largest lake in the Lesser Caucasus range.
Climate	Highland continental; hot summers, cold winters	Look for the golden summer light around 3:00–4:00 p.m.
Economy	Agriculture 17.2% Industry 36.4% Services 46.4% (est.)	Natural resources: small deposits of gold, copper, molybdenum, zinc, bauxite
Currency	Dram (AMD)	1 dram = 100 luma
Population	2,967,004 (2009 est.); 64% of pop. live in towns and cities	Pop. growth -0.03% (2009 est.). Decline due in part to emigration to Armenian diaspora across the globe
Life Expectancy	72.68 years (av.)	

Ethnic Makeup	Armenian (97.9%). Minorities incl. Yazidi (Kurd), Molokan (Russian)	
Language	Armenian. Russian is very widely spoken.	Signage also often in Russian and English
Literacy	99.4%	
Life Expectancy	72.68 years	
Religion	Armenian Apostolic Church is the official Church	"The first Christian nation"
Government	Presidential representative democratic republic. Directly elected president is the head of government and appoints the prime minister	Universal suffrage at 18 years. The unicameral parliament (Azgayin Zhoghov) has 131 seats. There are 11 provinces, or *marzer* (singular *marz*).
Media	Newspaper circulations are small; television much more popular	Government intervention still an issue
Electricity	220 volts, 50 hz	Electric outlets in Armenia use European plugs with two round prongs.
Video/TV	SECAM	
Telephone	Country code: 374 Yerevan city code: 10	To call a US number, dial 001+area code and number
Internet Domain	.am	
Time Zone	4 hours ahead of Greenwich Mean Time (GMT + 4)	Daylight saving (GMT + 5)

LAND &
PEOPLE

LOCATION

Armenia is a landlocked country in the southern
Caucasus. At 11,500 square miles (about 30,000
square kilometers) it is just 10 percent of its size in
the glory days of the ancient Kingdom of Armenia
(190 BCE to 387 CE).

An advertisement for Armenian tourism
proclaims, "Noah's Route, Your Route," a reference
to snowcapped Mount Ararat, which is highly
visible from Armenia's capital city of Yerevan.
It was here, according to the biblical Book of
Genesis, that Noah's Ark landed after the Flood
and life began again. For Armenians Mount
Ararat is a symbol of the unique nature of their
identity. It is part of their proud past, yet remains
a looming testimony to their loss, as this beloved
mountain now lies in Turkey.

Culturally, Armenia is considered neither East
nor West. Its language is an independent branch
of the Indo-European family—neither distinctly
Asian nor European. It has sealed borders with
two of its neighbors, and its very shape seems to
indicate unease with its current status. One
immediately notices that its southerly part divides
Azerbaijan. To the north of this is the kidney-
shaped piece of land called Nagorno-Karabakh.

In the 1990s, this area was a war zone, where long and bloody battles erupted between Armenia and Azerbaijan. To the south is the Nakhchivan Autonomous Republic, which, although not geographically connected to Azerbaijan, is internationally recognized as part of it. Today, this tiny republic remains isolated from Azerbaijan and most of the region.

To the west and south, the border with Turkey was closed as part of Turkey's solidarity with Azerbaijan during the Nagorno-Karabakh War of 1988–94, and has remained sealed. Armenians maintain that Turkey is using the closure to keep it isolated from important oil and transit lines, yet there are signs that this state of affairs may one day soften. In 2008, the Turkish president, Abdullah Gull, traveled to Yerevan to foster goodwill and attend a World Cup playoff between the two countries. Additionally, Turkey opened some airspace to Armenian airliners, allowing charter flights between Yerevan and Istanbul.

In 2009, talks began in earnest to create an Armenian–Turkish reconciliation.

Armenia relies on its open borders with Iran to the south and Georgia to the north. The Armenia–Georgia border is particularly important for trade with both Georgia and Russia. During the 2008 Russian–Georgian conflict, Armenians suffered shortages from fewer goods and services coming into their country—an indication of how dependent they remain on this open border. The border between Iran and Armenia continues to see the passage of both goods and people. Many Iranians come to Armenia: some are studying at the universities, and some are families wanting to avoid potential conflict brewing in their home country.

GEOGRAPHY

Armenia offers a diverse and intriguing landscape. In this small country can be found dry subtropics, semideserts, mountain steppes, forests, and pastoral meadows.

In the north of the country runs the range known as the Lesser Caucasus Mountains, which includes Armenia's highest point, Mount Aragats (13,418 feet, or 4,090 meters).

In contrast, the Ararat Valley, where the capital city of Yerevan is located, has the lowest elevations in the country and serves as its major agricultural region. Here, crops enjoy the longest duration of sunshine in the world (2,700 hours a year).

South of Yerevan, the Vayk and Zangezur mountain ranges run from north to south, bordering Nakhchivan. The Sunik range, also running from north to south, marks the border between Armenia and Azerbaijan.

The Armenian high plateau between the cities of Vayk and Goris is characterized by a treeless, rugged, mountainous region. Getting through it is difficult, but there are rewards in seeing this wild, almost untouched place.

Further south, the area around Kapan is dominated by Mount Khustup, whose peak is covered by fog for most of the time. In the southernmost part of the country, the region around the town of Meghri, near the border with Iran, is characterized by yet another climate zone. It is much warmer than the rest of Armenia, has a climate similar to Iran's, and is known for the cultivation of figs and the rare yellow pomegranate.

Another amazing feature of the country's natural environment is Lake Sevan, one of the largest alpine lakes in the world. It is both deep and wide, and spans 5 percent of Armenia's entire area.

The varied terrain provides the country with a diversity of plant and animal life that is quite rare

for such a small geographic space (and some Armenians say that this explains how Noah could collect so many species right here before the Flood). For example, Armenia has more than 365 bird species, compared to the 400 to 500 populating the entire European continent. The country also serves as an important migratory path for many animals and birds.

Armenia is still forming—it sits on highly active seismic terrain. A devastating earthquake in 1988 was a reminder of the volatility of the beautiful landscape that is part of this country.

CLIMATE

The Armenians regard the extremes of their climate as typical of the inconsistencies in their lives. In the course of a year, they experience all the pleasures and pains of the contrasts in their weather. The sunny patios around Yerevan's famous cafés, so popular in the summer, become treacherous icy surfaces, where people slip and fall in the freezing winter.

Winters in Yerevan can be particularly challenging. In January the temperature can drop to –5°F (–20°C). "Barely a molecule seems to move," said one visitor of a typical winter's day. Add to this situation the fact that many sidewalks are not shoveled or deiced, and it is easy to understand why schools and universities often close in early December and do not reopen until February.

Summers, on the other hand, are usually very hot, with temperatures in August climbing to 104°F (40°C). There is little rain during the summer months, and Yerevan can be very dry and dusty in July and August. However, a phenomenon that shouldn't be missed is the gold-tinged light of the Caucasus region on a summer afternoon. Around 3:00 p.m., one is treated to an amber glow that is uniquely special to this area of the world.

For those who want to be reminded of Armenia's ever-changing climate, a large and very visible digital thermometer sits atop the Opera House in the center of Yerevan. However, the accuracy of the reading is often a source of contention. It is rumored that neither extreme highs nor extreme lows are recorded, to avoid any requests from the populace for a day off work.

Armenians truly live "season by season." In the winter, there are the holiday festivities, but after these days pass most families stay secluded indoors. In spring there is a flurry of activity, and by summer it is time for tremendous outdoor social gatherings. It is as if Armenians store up their energies all winter for the social encounters that happen throughout the summer. In fact, visitors from Russia and other nearby countries often wait until July or August to travel to Armenia and take part in the café life of a Yerevan summer. Fall is a time for rain, and late in the season the rains can turn very cold. All those cafés start to close in October—a clear indication that the summertime fun is about to end.

THE PEOPLE

Where did the Armenian people originate? This question, too, is a topic of much discussion.

Of course there is the biblical story of Noah's Ark. Armenians say they are the descendants of Japheth, son of Noah. According to legend, after the Ark landed, Noah's family first settled in Armenia and then moved south to Babylon.

The fifth-century scholar Khorenatsi described Armenia's founding father, Haik, a descendant of Japheth, as a strong, handsome man with dark eyes and curly hair, who rebelled against the tyranny of Babylon and led a return to the land of Ararat. Haik was pursued by Bel, the wicked Babylonian ruler, whom he killed with a lucky arrow, after which he brought his people safely to the land of Ararat—dated to around 2490 BCE. Today, Armenians call themselves Hai, or Hay (pronounced "high"), and their country Haik or Hayastan, in honor of Haik.

Beside the biblical tales and legends, there is ample physical evidence of ancient cultures in the mountainous areas of the country. The earliest record to identify the Armenian people is an inscription from around 2300 BCE that mentions an attack on the "Armani" of the southern Armenian Highland. Another inscription, of Pharaoh Thutmose III of Egypt, refers to the people of "Ermenen" in 1446 BCE.

During the Bronze Age several states flourished in Greater Armenia. These included the Mitanni (in southwestern historical Armenia, around 1400 BCE), the Hittites (around 1300 BCE), Hayasa-

Azzi (1600–1200 BCE), Nairi (1400–1000 BCE), and the Kingdom of Urartu (1000–600 BCE). Each of these nations and tribes contributed to the formation of the Armenian people. Yerevan (then known as "Erebouni") was founded in 782 BCE by Argishti I, King of Urartu. Many artifacts from the Urartian civilization are on display in the Armenian History Museum.

The Armenian Diaspora

The Armenian Diaspora (those living outside the country) is much larger than the population within the country. Their influence looms in the lives of almost all who reside in the homeland. Although emigration had occurred long before, the twentieth century saw several massive flights to other countries. The century's first large-scale exodus occurred after the genocide of 1915–16. Others fled during Soviet times or were part of Stalin's deportation. Even more were driven to leave by the hardships of the early 1990s.

The relationship between Armenians and their Diaspora cousins is complicated. The country has long looked to its Diaspora to provide investments in the homeland, remittances, and various forms of assistance. Similarly, the people of the Diaspora turn to Armenia for inspiration as they strive to preserve their cultural identity far from the homeland.

Armenians have both respect for and reservations about the Diaspora. Many are appreciative of the funds that continue to flow to the country. Others see this population as those who did not suffer through the worst of times and therefore cannot truly understand their situation.

In the late 1990s, several efforts were made to strengthen relationships between Armenia and its Diaspora. The Pan Armenian Games were established to bring Diasporan athletes together. A Ministry of Diaspora Affairs was established by the Armenian government to help foster better relations and improve opportunities for trade. Also, in 2005, the Armenian government lifted a ban on dual citizenship.

A BRIEF HISTORY

Following the course of Armenian history is like watching a soccer game where the ball goes from one side of the field to the other. At times, the country is dominated by the West. At other times, it is ruled by the East. All of these back-and-forths naturally left their marks on the country and its culture. What is most impressive, however, is that these external influences remain just that—influences. Throughout it all, the Armenians have held firmly to their national identity.

The Very Beginning

We have already mentioned Haik, the descendant of Noah and the hero attributed with bringing the Armenian people back to their homeland. One of Haik's descendants six generations later was said to be Aram, a military leader who expanded the borders of his country and brought his nation to power. During his reign, the Greeks and Persians began to refer to the land as Aram's country, thus one interpretation of the origin of the name "Armenia."

Around 600 BCE, the Kingdom of Armenia was established under the Orontid Dynasty. In the course of its history, the kingdom would enjoy periods of independence, interrupted by periods of local autonomy subject to contemporary empires.

In around 520 BCE, Armenia became a satrapy (protectorate) of the Achaemenid (Persian) Empire under Darius I. During the next few centuries, Armenian troops fought for Persia in many major historic battles. The Armenian cavalry was well-known, especially during the reign of Vahe, a member of the later Haik Dynasty. Vahe was killed in 331 BCE while fighting for Persia in a battle against Alexander the Great.

After this battle, Armenia became a Hellenistic state, and in time would become part of the Hellenistic Empire founded by Alexander's general Seleucus. In around 200 BCE, the Seleucid king Antiochus appointed Artashes (also known as Artaxias) as the ruler of Greater Armenia. However, after Antiochus's defeat by the Romans at the battle of Magnesia in 190 BCE, Artashes and Zareh, his coruler in Lesser Armenia, revolted and, with Roman consent, began to reign autonomously with the title of King: Artashes over Greater Armenia and Zareh over Lesser Armenia.

From 95 to 55 BCE, under the long rule of Tigranes II (also known as Tigran the Great), Armenia was a powerful independent and united state, stretching from "sea to sea"—the Caspian Sea to the Mediterranean.

However, the size and power of Armenia did not go unnoticed by Rome. With the eastward expansion of the Romans during the Mithridatic Wars, Pompey defeated Tigranes and made Armenia a Roman protectorate in 66 BCE. For the next hundred years, Armenia remained under Roman influence. Then, Persia began to show renewed interest in the region and tensions rose. For years, Armenia was caught in the fighting between the two empires as each attempted to set up rulers who would become loyal to them. In 387 CE the area was officially split in two. Western Armenia became a province of the Roman Empire; Eastern Armenia remained a client kingdom of Persia until 428, when it became a marzpanate (governor generalship) of the Sassanian Persian dynasty.

The Golden Age
Meanwhile, another powerful force—Christianity—was entering Armenia. It would prove more lasting than either the Romans or the Persians. The apostles Thaddeus and Bartholomew traveled through the area and are credited with Armenia's early acceptance of Christianity. During their journeys they converted

many people and developed numerous secret Christian communities. In 301, St. Gregory the Illuminator baptized King Tiridates III of Armenia, who established Christianity as the official religion of the country. All pagan temples were destroyed—to this day, only one remains, in the village of Garni.

Armenians consider the time of the country's conversion to be a very sacred era. According to legend, St. Gregory had a vision that Christ himself descended into the Ararat Valley and struck the ground with a golden hammer to show where the first cathedral— St. Echmiadzin— should be built. Today this is the official center of the Holy Armenian Apostolic Church.

During the early days of Christianity in Armenia, masses were sung in Greek. However, this was not acceptable to the king, who wanted to develop and promote the Armenian language. He assigned the task to the scholarly monk and linguistic genius Mesrob Mashtots. The monk spent many years reviewing ancient Armenian scrolls in an effort to reconstruct the language and develop a distinct alphabet. In the end, he not only succeeded in creating a language, but also provided one of the first translations of the Bible

into a modern language. His biblical translation is considered one of the best in history.

But the golden age would not last. During the next two hundred years, a number of wars and skirmishes occurred. During the War of St. Vardan in 451, the Sassanian Persian King Yazdegerd II tried to suppress Christianity in Armenia and replace it with Zoroastrianism. The Armenians rallied against the Persian priests, who attempted to build temples and instill practices such as fire worship. A bloody battle took place and 66,000 Armenians, including St. Vardan, fought heroically until they were defeated by the much bigger Persian army. This lives on as the first documented war for the Christian faith.

In the seventh century the Persian Empire yielded regional control to invading Arab armies. Armenia came under Arab rule in 645 and experienced a degree of religious autonomy. As an autonomous principality within the Arab Empire, its Prince was recognized by both the Caliph and the Byzantine Emperor. Eventually, under the Bagratid kings Ashot I (862–90 CE) and Ashot II (952–77 CE), independence was regained and Armenia embarked on a second golden age. For years, the kingdom remained autonomous by playing the Arabs and their Byzantine rivals off against each other.

Neither would this golden age last forever. In the eleventh century, the Byzantines invaded from the west and the Seljuk Turks from the east, and the independent kingdoms in Armenia collapsed. A group of exiles founded a new state along the northeastern shore of the Mediterranean, known as the Armenian Kingdom of Cilicia (or Little or Lesser Armenia). This state was well-known for the round towers of its architecture and its alliance with the European crusaders. Cilician Armenia fought against the Muslims on behalf of Christian Europe until falling to a new wave of Turks from Central Asia in 1375.

In the thirteenth century Caucasian Armenia suffered invasions by Mongols and other Central Asian tribes. In the fourteenth century the Ottoman Turks in Anatolia expanded at the expense of the Byzantine Empire, and eventually captured Constantinople in 1453. Between the sixteenth and the eighteenth centuries Caucasian Armenia was divided between the Ottomans and the Safavid Persians.

Russians and Turks

In the eighteenth century, a new player in the tug-of-war for Armenia came on the scene: Russia. Although largely under Turkish and Persian rule in the early eighteenth century, the Armenians started looking toward the growing Russian power for assistance. Several messengers were sent to the Russian tsars to ask for protection from the Turks. The wealthy Armenian trading community of New Julfa in Isfahan even made Tsar Alexis I Mikhailovich a gift of a throne adorned with gold and precious stones to win his favor. However, the call for help remained largely unanswered, as were requests made to other European nations to help "a fellow Christian country."

Finally, there was a ray of hope in the 1800s, when Georgia and Karabakh came under Russian rule. A series of revolts by its non-Turkish communities had erupted throughout the declining Ottoman Empire. The fall of the Empire seemed likely, and Tsar Nicholas I started to make more aggressive moves to take advantage of the situation. During the Russo–Turkish war of 1828–29, his forces came within forty-five miles (72 km) of Constantinople, and the Turkish Sultan sued for peace. The Treaty of Adrianople gave Russia sovereignty over Georgia and parts of present-day Armenia.

The treatment of Armenians and their rights under the neighboring Ottoman Empire began to be known in European diplomatic circles as "the Armenian question." This issue grew in world importance during the later Russo–Turkish War of 1877–78, as the plight of the Armenians came under international scrutiny.

Notwithstanding this attention, the situation worsened for those Armenians under Turkish rule. From 1894 to 1896, systematic massacres were ordered by Turkey's Sultan Abdul-Hamid II. The Sultan (whose own mother, ironically, was said to be Armenian) considered the Armenian population a threat that would provide a pretext for European and Russian interference. The Turkish government engineered assaults on Armenian villages that spread throughout the area and into almost all of Western Armenia. Many Armenian villages organized armed resistance, but it was not enough to halt the bloody pogroms that resulted in the death of tens or even hundreds of thousands of Armenians— figures range from 100,000 to 300,000.

During the Sultan's reign, an opposition reform party known as the Young Turks began gaining momentum in the Ottoman Empire. With their slogan of "fraternity and common homeland," the Young Turks even attracted a few Armenians, who believed in their promise of an "autonomous Western Armenia." In fact, some Armenians helped to finance their campaigns against the Sultan. After the Young Turk Revolution of

1908, the Sultan's successor, Muhammad V, was reduced to a powerless symbolic figure.

The victory of the Young Turks did not, however, mitigate the Armenians' troubles. In 1909, Turkish mobs attacked Armenians in a series of bloody rampages in Adana and Cilicia. The Turkish military sent in to restore order were reported to have participated in the violence.

As Turkey entered the Balkan Wars of 1912–13 with Bulgaria, Serbia, Greece, and Montenegro, widespread nationalism fomented greater animosity against the Armenian population in the Ottoman Empire. Armenians were regarded as dangerous elements. Armenian bankers were accused of stealing from the state, Armenian businesses were boycotted, and rumors flew about of an Armenian underground organization attempting to destroy the country.

The Armenian Genocide

The Armenian Genocide started on April 24, 1915. On this day 250 Armenian leaders were arrested and killed in Constantinople. Also in April 1915, Turkish troops began attacks on the Armenian city of Van. Under the leadership of Aram Manukiahe, the Armenians attempted to defend themselves—a defense that lasted thirty-six days and resulted in 55,000 Armenian deaths. Armenian volunteer soldiers serving in the Tsarist Russian army rescued the survivors.

After what the Turks called "The Revolution of Van," the Armenians were declared "internal enemies" of the Ottoman Empire. Within a year, mass deportation of the Armenian population began, and the Turkish government passed a law stating that the authorities would confiscate all property, livestock, and homes belonging to Armenians. During this time, many Armenians were not only forced to give up their homes, but hundreds of thousands were sent on death marches and brutally murdered. According to the *New York Times*, the roads were, "strewn with corpses of exiles, and those who survive are doomed to certain death. It is a plan to exterminate the whole Armenian people." In total, 1.5 million Armenians are estimated to have died in 1915–16.

800,000 ARMENIANS COUNTED DESTROYED

Viscount Bryce Tells House of Lords That Is the Probable Number of Turks' Victims.

10,000 DROWNED AT ONCE

Peers Are Told How Entire Christian Population of Trebizond Was Wiped Out.

APRIL 24: REMEMBERING THE GENOCIDE

The genocide that occurred at the turn of the last century has had a powerful impact on surviving generations, both within the country and abroad. It is a lasting reminder to Armenian sons and daughters that they must preserve their culture and their people.

April 24 is considered worldwide Armenian Genocide Remembrance Day. It was first commemorated in 1965, when thousands of Armenians staged a twenty-four-hour demonstration in the streets of Yerevan. Soviet troops attempted to restore order as the impassioned crowd shouted, "Our land, our land!" However, to prevent this type of demonstration from happening again, the Kremlin agreed to build a memorial complex in honor of genocide victims. By 1967, the memorial was completed at Tsitsernakaberd, above the Hrazdan Gorge in Yerevan.

Remembrance of the genocide occurs across the globe. Genocide Remembrance Day events take place in Europe and North and South America every year. Armenian genocide memorials have been built in many countries, including France, the USA, Lebanon, Uruguay, and Venezuela. Ongoing studies of the genocide, its aftermath, and global lessons are conducted in many universities.

Yet, recognition of the fact of genocide is still a point of contention in some countries. Many countries are concerned about offending Turkey (which claims that both sides suffered losses during a time of war) and several of its allies, and have not officially condemned the act. In 2006, the USA dismissed its ambassador to Armenia, purportedly for remarks made in favor of Armenia and recognition of the genocide. In 2009, US President Barack Obama addressed the Turkish parliament and sidestepped use of the word "genocide," referring instead to "the terrible events of 1915."

In 2007 Hrant Dink, the Turkish–Armenian editor of the newspaper *Agos*, was assassinated after criticizing Turkey's steadfast denial that there ever had been a genocide. Dink remains a prominent Armenian hero. At his funeral in Istanbul thousands of mourners proclaimed, "We are all Armenians," and "We are all Hrant Dink."

Reenter the Russians

In 1916 most of Ottoman Armenia was conquered by Tsarist Russia, but these gains were lost with the Bolshevik Revolution of 1917. During the same period, a group of Armenians living further north in Tbilisi were forming the Armenian Revolutionary Federation. They were strong advocates of socialism and vehement Armenian nationalists, and worked to unify small groups of Armenians throughout the region and defend Armenian villages. Additionally, in 1918, the ARF was instrumental in the creation of an independent state, the Democratic Republic of Armenia (DRA), which was supported by the victorious Allied powers.

Independence was short-lived. In 1920, forces of Mustafa Kemal Ataturk's Turkish National Movement invaded from the east, and the Turkish–Armenian War broke out. At about the same time, there were Communist uprisings within the DRA. At the end of the year, the Red Army began to invade the region. Exhausted from years of war and attempting to care for the needs of thousands of Armenian refugees from the former Ottoman Empire, the embattled new nation could no longer resist. On December 4, 1920, the Red Army entered Yerevan. By 1922, Armenia became part of the Transcaucasian Soviet Socialist Republic, consisting of Armenia, Georgia, and Azerbaijan. Western Armenia remained part of Turkey and northwestern Iran.

On October 13, 1921, the Kars treaty was signed between Turkey and the Socialist Republics of Azerbaijan, Armenia, and Georgia. This treaty augmented the earlier Moscow treaty (signed on March 16, 1921) between Bolshevist Russia and Kemalist Turkey. It established the present borders between Turkey and Armenia, ceding to Turkey areas acquired by Imperial Russia from the Ottoman Empire during the Russo–Turkish War of 1877–78. Most significantly, Mount Ararat—the beloved symbol of the Armenian nation—was ceded to Turkey.

In 1936, the Transcaucasian Republic was dissolved and Armenia became one of fifteen constituent Socialist Republics of the Soviet Union. Like the other Republics, Armenia was governed by the Central Committee of the Republican Communist Party.

Armenia Under the Soviets

In the 1930s, Armenians, like all ethnic minorities within the Soviet Union, suffered the persecutions and mass deportations launched by Joseph Stalin. Almost every Armenian family was touched by his brutality. Any efforts at developing Armenian arts and sciences were suppressed, and many prominent Armenian writers, artists, scientists, and political leaders were executed or forced into exile. In 1936, Stalin began deporting Armenians to Siberia in a reported attempt to reduce Armenia's population and engineer its annexation by his native Georgia.

Additionally, the Soviet government began measures to persecute the Armenian Apostolic Church, which had already been weakened by the genocide. Khoren Muradpekyan (known as Koren I), the leader of the Armenian Church, was killed,

and the Cathedral of
Echmiadzin was closed.
It is said that if not for the
Armenian Diaspora, the
Armenian Church would not
have survived this period.

Soon, the Second World
War diverted Stalin's
attention. Although the Nazis
had intended to capture the
oil fields of Azerbaijan, they
never made it to the South Caucasus area.
However, Armenia played an extremely valuable
role in aiding the Allies. More than 500,000
Armenians fought in the war, and close to half
of these troops lost their lives.

Armenians of the Soviet 89th "Tamanyan"
Division fought in fierce battles against the
Germans in the Battle of the Caucasus, the Battle
of the Crimea, the Battle of the Baltic, the Vistula-
Oder Offensive, and the Battle of Berlin. Senior
Sergeants Hunan Avetisyan and S. Arakelyan
earned the rank of Hero of the Soviet Union
during an attack on the German-held city of
Novorossiysk. The award to Avetisyan was made
posthumously after he had thrown himself into
the path of the Germans, killing himself but
saving his squad so that they could advance.

One of the greatest war heroes was General
Hovannes (Ivan) Baghramian, who later became
a Marshal of the Soviet Union. Baghramian was
the first non-Slavic officer to become a front
commander in 1944. His forces took back the
Baltic republics captured by the Germans

earlier in the war and liberated hundreds of towns in Poland and the former Czechoslovakia. Today, a major street in Yerevan is named after him, and a statue of this greatly revered hero stands at the foot of the American University Armenia. Another monument to Second World War heroes, Victory Bridge, spans the Hrazdan River in Yerevan. Built in 1945, it was named in honor of those who fought in the "Great Patriotic War."

At the end of the Second World War, many Armenians lobbied Stalin to take back parts of western Turkey. Although Stalin initiated some saber rattling, the effort was quickly countered by President Truman, who warned that he would assist any country threatened by "Soviet aggression." The Kremlin quickly halted the movement.

Also after the war, Stalin initiated a more open immigration policy in Armenia. He offered to pay for Diasporans to come back to the country, settle, revitalize the population, and join its workforce. As a result, Armenia saw an influx of more than 150,000 Diasporans, survivors of the genocide, or their descendants, who had been living in France, Greece, Iraq, Lebanon, and Syria. However, the welcome did not last very long. In the late 1940s, Stalin launched a new campaign of terror, and thousands of Armenians were arrested and deported to Siberia.

National Reawakening

Following a power struggle after Stalin's death in 1953, Nikita Khrushchev started a process of de-Stalinization, attempting to restore normality and order to the area. He put more resources into the production of consumer goods and housing, Yerevan's population grew, and the overall economy improved. Limited religious freedoms were granted, and the arts began to flourish. One of Khrushchev's advisers and close friends, the Armenian politburo member Anastas Ivanovich Mikoyan, urged Armenians to rediscover their classic writers and artists. The Soviet Armenian composer Aram Khachaturyan also created his greatest works at this time.

The rebirth experienced during the Khrushchev era came to an end under Brezhnev, who was helped to power by Mikoyan. The Brezhnev period of the 1970s was marked by economic stagnation, a decline in goods and services, and worsening housing conditions. Although Moscow loosened central control over the area, the local party officials became more powerful and imparted their own brand of bribery and corruption.

The remnants of the Brezhnev era are abundant to this day in contemporary Yerevan. Large Soviet-style concrete apartment blocks still stand throughout the city, and the building that currently houses part of the American University Armenia is a former Communist Party meeting hall. Large and imposing, it is a reminder of the privileges enjoyed by those who were well entrenched in the Soviet government.

In 1987, cracks in the Soviet system were readily apparent. The Soviet leader Mikhail Gorbachev openly criticized Party operations in Armenia, accusing the local government of being "stuck in a rut." His policy of *glasnost* (openness) encouraged the growth of national sentiment.

The final straw came on December 7, 1988, when an earthquake devastated northern Armenia, killing at least 25,000, including many health care workers in poorly constructed hospitals left over from the Brezhnev era, and leaving more than 500,000 people homeless. Large amounts of direct aid came from the Diaspora. Moscow, however, was noticeably unresponsive.

Independent Armenia

The Soviet government was officially disbanded in August 1991, and a referendum for independence was held in Armenia on September 21, 1991. The Armenians voted overwhelmingly for independence from the Soviet Union. On the very same day, American University Armenia opened its doors in Yerevan. In October 1991, Levon Ter-Petrossian became the first popularly elected president in Armenian history. Lenin Square, the city's main square, was renamed Republic Square, and Lenin's statue was toppled. (If you want to see the now headless statue, it is said you can ask the curators of the National History Museum.)

The joy of independence was short-lived. Armenia's ongoing dispute over the Nagorno-Karabakh region was coming to a head. In 1990, anti-Armenian pogroms had taken place in the Azerbaijani capital, Baku, killing about ninety people and forcing most Armenians to flee the city. Then, as Armenia and Azerbaijan declared their independence from Russia, Nagorno-Karabakh declared itself free from Azerbaijan.

NAGORNO-KARABAKH: THE FROZEN WAR

In the 1930s, Stalin separated Nagorno-Karabakh—a majority Armenian region—from Armenia and gave it to neighboring Azerbaijan, creating regional tensions that remain unresolved. In the late 1980s, an Azeri-led pogrom targeted at Armenians in the town of Sumgait brought the situation to the boiling point.

When the Soviet Union collapsed, Armenia and Azerbaijan declared their independence from Russia, and Nagorno-Karabakh declared its independence from Azerbaijan. Soon after, war broke out between Azerbaijan and Armenia over Nagorno-Karabakh.

Although better armed, the Azerbaijani forces lost ground to the Armenians. By the time a Russian-brokered truce took hold, Armenia had taken control not only of Nagorno-Karabakh, but also of parts of Azerbaijan.

The conflict over Nagorno-Karabakh is considered a "frozen war." There are ongoing military exchanges between Azerbaijani and Armenian forces. Also, it is one of the central issues in the dispute between Armenia and Turkey. (Turkey sides with Azerbaijan.) Russian troops remain in Armenia to guard the country against Turkey.

Armenians are intensely passionate about the Nagorno-Karabakh issue. Many lost loved ones in the conflict, and they consider it extremely important to their country to retain the region.

In the late winter of 1992, international mediation failed to bring a resolution. By the spring of 1993, Armenian forces captured several key regions of Nagorno-Karabakh and in 1994, the Armenians were in full control of the territory, along with some surrounding land in Azerbaijan. As a result of this conflict, hundreds of thousands of Armenians were displaced from Azerbaijan and even more Azeris were forced to leave Armenia and Karabakh. A Russian-brokered cease-fire was signed in May 1994, but relations between Armenia and Azerbaijan have been frozen ever since.

The war took a terrible toll on Armenians back home. During the conflict, Turkey joined Azerbaijan in sealing its borders with Armenia and huge shortages occurred, effectively crippling the economy. Electricity and water supplies were affected, often being limited to just a few hours a day even during the coldest part of winter.

Compounding this situation was the fact that Armenia's Soviet-led industry had almost ground to a halt after independence. The nation's industrial output dropped by nearly 64 percent. Most social welfare programs stopped, and many families were left to fend for themselves. People in Yerevan cut down trees for fuel, and the antiquated nuclear power plant at Metsamor was started up again, despite warnings that it had become unsafe after the 1988 earthquake.

During this troubling time, hundreds of thousands of Armenians emigrated. Many went to Russia to find work and escape the dreadful conditions, but others left for Europe and the United States. California was especially appealing as George

Deukmejian, the son of Armenian immigrants, served as the state's governor from 1983 to 1991.

It took several years to recover from war and the blockade, and by the beginning of the twenty-first century Armenia had begun to show signs of economic recovery. Much of the early growth depended on external support—remittances from the Diaspora and assistance from international organizations. However, a significant construction

boom began in the early years of the new century and helped to drive up the gross domestic product. Cranes dominated the skyline and ultramodern high-rises soared above the center of Yerevan.

Whether the boom will continue, and whether buildings will be fully occupied, remains to be seen.

GOVERNMENT AND POLITICS

The Constitution of Armenia, adopted in 1995, established it as a presidential democratic republic with universal suffrage for all citizens over the age of eighteen. The president is elected by popular vote for a five-year term. There is a unicameral parliament, the Azgayin Zhoghov, or National Assembly. Of its 131 seats, 90 members are elected by party list and 41 directly. The prime minister is appointed by the president on the basis of representation in the National Assembly.

In 2009 the government consisted of a coalition of four political parties: the conservative

Republican Party of Armenia (HHK), Prosperous Armenia, the Armenian Revolutionary Federation ("Dashnak" or ARF), and the Rule of Law Party. The main opposition Heritage Party favors eventual membership of the European Union and NATO.

Armenians feel both cynical and hopeful about their government. As the country inches toward true democracy, it has experienced assassinations on the floor of Parliament, violent protests, and repeated claims of voter fraud. Yet Armenians continue to press for a more democratic rule.

The height of political turmoil occurred on October 27, 1999, when, after a decade of unrest, the Prime Minister, Vazgen Sargsyan, and the Parliament Speaker, Karen Demirchyan, along with six other officials, were assassinated in the parliament building. This act began a period of protest and instability during which there were several unsuccessful attempts by the opposition party to force President Robert Kocharyan to resign.

Kocharyan was reelected in 2003, but began his term with allegations of ballot fraud. In early 2004, protesters once again took to the streets with calls for his resignation. However, his party remained in office.

Again, turmoil erupted in 2008 with the election of the Kocharyan-backed Serzh Sargsyan. The opposition, supporting former President Levon Ter-Petrossian, again disputed the results and protested for more than a week in Yerevan. On March 1, 2008, violence broke out between the police and protesters, leaving at least ten people dead. A state of emergency was imposed for twenty days. A year later, more than 10,000 people gathered in central Yerevan to stage a peaceful rally in memory of the dead.

chapter two

VALUES &
ATTITUDES

Who invented positron emission tomography (PET) scanning? Who was the world's chess champion for years? Who owned more than thirty airports? Who won eight grand slam singles tennis tournaments and an Olympic gold medal? Who sold more than 275 million records worldwide and is one of the world's best-known pop stars? You probably know the answer already. An Armenian!

National pride runs very deep. Almost every Armenian can name a litany of accomplished countrymen: Michel (Michael) Ter-Pogossian, inventor of the PET scanner; chess champion Gary Kasparov; billionaire Eduardo Eurnekian; tennis champion Andre Agassi; and singer Cher, to mention just a very few.

But it is more than just the fact that these individuals share a common background (and often a "ian" or "yan" suffix to their name). Because these people are Armenians, therefore they are family. And to be part of an Armenian family that has shared joy and suffering together is the most important thing of all.

Although there are many characteristics that define what it is to be Armenian, the most prominent are family, education, hospitality, and intense national pride.

THE FAMILY

In America, a television reality show called "Keeping Up with the Kardashians" depicted the exploits of an Armenian-American Diaspora family in Los Angeles. The show was filled with racy adventures such as the oldest daughter posing for *Playboy* (with her mother's blessing). Suffice it to say, this is *not* a typical Armenian family!

The typical family living in Armenia maintains conservative, traditional values. Women marry in their early or mid twenties and men only slightly later in life. Typically, they will have two or three children and their marriages will last for life. Divorce and separation, although legal, are still considered somewhat taboo.

The pull of the family is extremely strong. Young married men often bring their brides home and live under the parental roof for several years. This may come about for economic reasons, but it is also important to stay close to loved ones. As one Armenian states, "People are not supposed to be alone." Thus, the typical Armenian is always surrounded by aunts, uncles, cousins, and other relatives throughout his or her life. "Family is what makes us comfortable," says another.

Children learn the importance of family at a very early age. Within each household, life nearly always revolves around the children, and the family provides them with attention, acceptance, and plenty of affection. Although their mothers primarily raise them, they are also doted on by their grandmothers, cousins, and aunts. When they are born they are bestowed with gifts. As they grow, birthdays are celebrated and, of course, family parties are attended by many, many relatives.

The family also offers protection. In Armenia, children are protected and looked after well into their teen years—far later in life than in some Western countries. Most would never be left "home alone" without some form of adult supervision, even into their late teens.

Leaving the family is considered a very big move, and is done only with the family's blessing. Dating is allowed, but often only under supervision—one sees many couples stealing a furtive cuddle on the steps of the Cascade in Yerevan and other out-of-eyeshot locations. Friendships between young men and women are still viewed somewhat suspiciously, especially by the older generations, who do not understand how young people can be "just friends." To the elders, a man and a woman together should mean only one thing—they intend to start a family.

Even later in life, Armenian men and women typically separate off, and even married couples tend to keep with their own sex when socializing, on the subway, or in their day-to-day activities.

EDUCATION

Education is extremely important in Armenian culture—so important that, during the harsh early years of independence, while all other social services collapsed, the education system remained intact. To be educated is to be able to fulfill the hopes of one's family and one's country. All boys and girls are expected to go to school and do very well in their studies. Early in the morning in Yerevan, you'll see children, in crisp blue and white uniforms, walking eagerly to school, many of them hand-in-hand with their parents.

With schooling so important to the culture, Armenia has an extremely high literacy rate. Today, it is estimated at 99.4 percent. School attendance is high in both urban and rural areas, and approximately 80 percent of all students complete high school. College is a goal for many Armenian students, both male and female.

HOSPITALITY

In the center of the traffic circle in Yerevan's Republic Square is a large oval surface. Although you will have to negotiate the madly circling taxis, it's worth trying to take a look. Etched in the cement oval is the pattern of an Armenian rug— the kind placed in most living rooms to welcome guests—which symbolizes the world-renowned hospitality of the Armenian people.

In a sense, Armenian hospitality is an extension of the regard for family. In a culture where "family" extends to aunts, uncles, cousins, and far beyond, many are welcomed within this warm embrace.

Armenians famously open up their homes and share their time with others on a regular basis. The spirit of hospitality is pervasive throughout the country, but especially in rural areas, where it is quite common for visitors to be invited into homes for coffee, a taste of homemade wine, or even a meal.

In Yerevan, it is not quite as common to be invited into a family home, but there is a spirit of welcome that is unmatched in other cities. Tourists will notice this friendliness, as they are almost always stopped on the street and asked if they need directions, assistance, or—sometimes—a good dinner.

ATTITUDES TOWARD WOMEN

Perhaps one of the most complex and often discussed part of traditional Armenian culture is the woman's role. A highly traditional society, Armenia harbors many old-fashioned attitudes about the role

of women, and even today there is some pressure for women to conform. However, this situation is changing with a new generation of Armenians who are also rethinking old attitudes toward male–female relationships.

In traditional families, a boy is treated very differently from his sisters. He is the prince of the household, and is not expected to participate in most chores. A female relative will clean up after him.

Once a man, the traditional Armenian male becomes the king of the household. He is responsible for the family income, and the major economic decisions such as buying a home or a car are in his domain. Women, on the other hand, have the responsibility of cooking, cleaning, and raising the children. The kitchen is generally off-limits to the men, since this is where a traditional Armenian woman is expected to excel. It is a great honor for an Armenian woman to be asked for a recipe by another woman who is known to be a good cook.

To the foreign observer, these roles may seem somewhat limiting for the women. In a very traditional household it is not uncommon for the man to tell the woman when she can go out with her friends and when she must stay at home to tend to the house and family. Even with a dating couple, the boy can dictate the activities of his girlfriend.

Additionally, one notices the women working very hard. During the day, women are seen staffing stores and offices. At 6:00 p.m., they rush to buy food in the markets and run home to prepare meals, do the laundry, tend to the children, and clean the house. Men, on the other hand, linger on street corners, talk with friends or business associates, smoke, and eventually make their way home, where they know food will be on the table.

To be fair, one should mention a few important factors. Lack of employment has forced many men to leave the country and find work in Russia (travel on a flight from Yerevan to Moscow and you will immediately notice that most of the passengers are male). Therefore, seeing women doing "a lot of things" is understandable, as they are the predominant sex, and the intense "double duty" performed by women throughout the day is nothing new. In Soviet times, women were expected to serve as comrades in the workforce as well as maintain a well-run household.

The Busybody

Because Armenia is such a close-knit society, it has given rise to the most annoying figure in the neighborhood—the local busybody. Almost every apartment block has one and she—it is usually a woman—is feared and reviled, especially by young people. In the words of one young woman, "This is the only thing I cannot stand about Armenia. The neighborhood busybody knows everything that you are doing."

Armenians tend to be more judgmental of themselves than of foreigners. The kind of behavior that is tolerated in outsiders, such as kissing in public, wearing revealing clothing, and being drunk in public, is not acceptable for Armenians—particularly young people. If a young person is seen coming home too late or engaging in public displays of affection with a boyfriend or girlfriend, it will assuredly be reported back home by the busybody.

Finally, attitudes are changing. The women who populate many of the colleges and universities are highly aware that they are a generation in flux. Whereas their mothers and fathers tended to stick with tradition, younger men and women are reexamining their roles. It is becoming increasingly common to see a young father playing with his children in the park or even taking them on a shopping excursion.

ATTITUDES TO HOMOSEXUALITY

Pressures to conform to traditional roles in Armenia understandably make gay life difficult. But there is some change occurring. Armenia has implemented several reforms to promote more tolerance of the lesbian, gay, bisexual, and transgender communities.

Chief among the latest reforms is repeal of Article 116 of 1936, which made homosexuality punishable by law. With the abolition of this law, a gay scene began to emerge in Yerevan. The first gay bar in the city was opened in 2004. Two gay rights NGOs recently registered within the country, including the Public Information and Need of Knowledge (PINK) center in Yerevan, which also maintains an informative Web site.

However, openly gay couples still find life difficult. Gay couples typically do not express intimacy in public. Although, paradoxically, people of the same sex often hold hands or kiss on greeting, these actions are considered part of tradition and not indicative of a gay lifestyle.

ETHNIC MINORITIES

In a land where less than 3 percent of the population is not ethnically Armenian, one can imagine that life is not always easy for those who are counted among the minorities. However, outright intolerance is extremely rare. This is especially true in Yerevan, where locals often go out of their way to be accommodating to those who do not look, or speak, Armenian.

The largest ethnic and religious minority in Armenia is the Yazidis, a Kurdish community who number about 40,000 in the west of the country. Many Yazidis came to Armenia and Georgia during the nineteenth and early twentieth centuries to escape religious persecution by the Ottoman Turks, who had tried to convert them from Yazidism— a monotheistic religion that incorporates many Jewish, Christian, and Muslim traditions—to Islam. Their story is similar to the Armenians', in that they were massacred alongside them during the genocide of the early twentieth century. Relationships with the Armenians are relatively stable, and the Yazidis have developed strong ties with the country. During the Nagorno-Karabakh War, members of the Yazidi community renounced their ties with the Muslim Kurds, and some took up arms in support of the Armenian army.

Another small minority, the Molokans, also have a historic alignment with Armenia. A religious sect made up predominantly of Russian peasants, Molokans broke from the Russian Orthodox Church in the 1550s. They got their name from the Russian word for milk (*moloko*), because they refused to participate in the Orthodox days of fasting, drinking milk instead. Molokans also follow Old Testament kosher dietary laws. They claim to be direct descendants from an ancient Armenian tribe that also migrated to Bulgaria, Bosnia, and Serbia.

Much has also been written about Jews in Armenia. The Jewish population began settling in the country around 80 BCE, when Tigranes the Great returned from Palestine with about 10,000 Jews. Today, very few of the Jewish community remain, and those who do are generally left in peace. However, the Jews, like all others who make up Armenia's minorities, are always aware that they are not a part of the majority of Armenians.

THE IMPORTANCE OF RELIGION

Ask any Armenian what sets his or her country apart, and you will almost always hear, "We were the first Christian nation." This distinction is very much a part of the national identity, regardless of whether or not one attends church on a regular basis.

The vast majority of Armenians (90 percent) adhere to the Armenian Apostolic Church, which is the official state religion. Although the country's constitution provides for freedom of religion for the small communities of non-Apostolic Church members, the state Church enjoys many privileges not available to other groups.

The Armenian Apostolic Church is an entirely separate religious entity unto itself. It severed ties with Rome and Constantinople in 554 after

rejecting the ruling about the nature of Christ proposed by the Council of Chalcedon. It is headed by its spiritual leader, the Catholicos of All Armenians, who is President of the Supreme Spiritual Council and the College of Bishops, and a central figure in Armenian culture. He resides in the town of Echmiadzin, whose cathedral was built in St. Gregory's time.

In the Soviet era, church attendance was widely discouraged, especially during Stalin's reign, when attempts were made to eliminate the Church. Koren I, the Catholicos at the time, was killed, and Echmiadzin Cathedral was shuttered. However, despite his reign of terror, Stalin could not sever the Armenians' ties to their Church, which survived thanks to an underground movement in Armenia and the faith of the Diaspora.

After Soviet rule, the country experienced a resurgence in religious fervor. In 1999, there were only a hundred priests in all of Armenia. Since then, the number has more than doubled. From seventeen pre-independence churches, there are now almost two hundred conducting worship in Armenia.

Although not all Armenians are actively involved in the Church (attendance is still relatively low), awareness of religion as part of the national identity is quite high—and likely to increase. And, as testimony to the endurance of the Church in Armenia, Yerevan's St. Gregory the Illuminator Cathedral was consecrated in 2001. It was built to celebrate the seventeen hundredth anniversary of Christianity in Armenia and, symbolically, it seats seventeen hundred people.

WEALTH AND MONEY

The image of the Armenian as a consummate businessperson goes back a long way. With seemingly endless confrontations from foreign rulers, and no real chance for political gains within their own country, the Armenians in the Middle Ages established a new class of leaders, both at home and abroad. These were the merchants and traders. They quickly gained a reputation as good businessmen, spreading literacy and culture wherever they went, from Europe to parts of Asia. Remarking on the Armenian influence in India, the French historian Fernand Braudel wrote, "Where would Madras be without the Armenians?"

The Armenian reputation for business also flourished along with the Diaspora. Today, many prominent businesspeople throughout the world can claim Armenian roots. And this special skill in business affairs remains a source of pride.

A Talent for Business

An Armenian man, named Artash, walked into a bank in New York City and asked for the loan officer. He told the officer that he was going to Yerevan on business for two weeks, and needed to borrow $5,000.

The officer told him that the bank would need some form of security for the loan. Artash handed over the keys to a new Ferrari parked on the street in front of the bank. He produced the title, everything checked out, the car was accepted as security, and Artash departed with his loan. The American bank's president and its officers all had a good laugh at the Armenian who offered a $250,000 car as collateral for a $5,000 loan, and an employee moved the Ferrari safely into the bank's underground garage.

Two weeks later, Artash returned and repaid the loan and the interest, which came to $15.41. The loan officer said, "Sir, we are very happy to have had your business, and this transaction has worked out very nicely, but we are a little confused. While you were away, we checked you out and found that you are a multimillionaire. What puzzles us is, why would you bother to borrow $5,000?"

Artash replied, "Where else in New York City can I park my car for two weeks for only $15.41 and expect it to be there when I return?"
Ah, the Armenian brain . . . This is why Hayastan is shining!

Within the homeland itself, however, opportunities for economic prosperity have been somewhat restricted. Genocide followed by the Soviet system stifled the Armenian flair for enterprise. Until the global recession of 2009, Armenia was striving to get back on its feet, and was doing so at a relatively fast pace. The average per capita gross domestic product in Armenia nearly tripled from 2000 to 2005, but it still remained at less than half the per capita GDP of its neighbors Georgia and Azerbaijan.

Armenians have a positive attitude toward the accumulation of wealth, and love tales of successful Armenian businesspeople. However, they are aware that the fabled business class has yet to experience resurgence in the homeland. For real success, modern Armenia must overcome significant economic vulnerabilities. First, economic growth is heavily reliant on increasing exports, which is obviously hampered by the closed borders. Also, exportable products and services are somewhat limited (for example, diamond polishing). Government, too, must loosen its grip on tariffs and taxation. To restore the economic pride of the past, Armenia needs greater investment, expansion of capital markets, and even further government and banking reforms.

A second vulnerability is the continued dependence on remittances from Armenians abroad. According to the International Monetary Fund (IMF) and the Central Bank of Armenia, remittances actually exceeded the country's annual budget. This widespread dependence also makes the country highly vulnerable to fluctuations in the global economy, as evidenced by how the country was hit by the global recession of 2009.

Also, there are vast differences in wealth across the country. Although Armenia's economy has improved, Yerevan, with one-third of the country's population, produces more than half of its gross domestic product. According to the United Nations Development Program Statistics, about half of Armenia's rural population of 1.5 million lives in poverty. The government, Diaspora groups, and nongovernment aid organizations have introduced several programs to relieve the dire situation in the rural areas; however, for many, the circumstances are still very serious.

And then there are the oligarchs. Just as in Russia, an enormously wealthy class of oligarchs has made its way to the top of society. Since independence, the rise of this new elite has hampered Armenian economic reform. These influential businessmen not only control key industries, but also sit in parliament. Many Armenians hope that reforms will one day loosen the oligarchs' grip on both business and government, but there is still much that can be done.

Oligarchs are not shy about showing their wealth. They build outrageously lavish mansions; they give their sons and daughters Mercedes cars when they turn sixteen; they frequent the upscale retail shops being built along Yerevan's North Avenue. Their muscle-bound "protectors" are well-known. These are not a revival of the

Armenian tradesmen of old; it is widely agreed that their influence on issues such as distribution of wealth, anticorruption, criminal justice reform, and privatization are harming progressive economic reforms in Armenia.

RUSSIAN INFLUENCE ON ARMENIAN SOCIETY

Many Western foreigners are surprised by how strongly the Armenians are tied to the Russians. Most of this closeness has been strategically engineered by the Russians, who are seen as the protectors against Azerbaijan. However, ties with Russia are deeper than even this political alliance.

Armenians feel very close to Russia. The products in stores are frequently manufactured in Russia. Russian television shows—especially cartoons—are extremely popular. Young people listen to Russian pop music, and are familiar with Russian celebrities. Going to a Russian university is a goal of many. And, should you become very ill, a hospital in Moscow is your destination.

Armenians say they have similar values to Russians, particularly when it comes to honoring one's family, pursuing an education, and viewing the world with a touch more skepticism than the more optimistic Westerner. If given a choice between Russia and a Western country, many Armenians would choose Russia because, as one native put it, "Russia is familiar to us."

Interestingly, all this closeness to Russia and, of course, a history of Communist bureaucracy, has influenced the Armenian psyche in some manner.

There are still those who cling to the old ways and believe that administration and bureaucracy trump customer service. Every once in a while, the foreigner will come in contact with the bristly, intractable side of Soviet-influenced Armenia. It occurs in the post office when one is told that something can't be done, and in the bank when a transaction is said to be "impossible." Sometimes the visitor will be saved by a native who simply cannot bear to watch this happen. However, should you get caught in such a situation and see no help in sight, it's best to move on, knowing that, although somewhat rare in its appearance, an obdurate side of Armenia exists.

THE DEFINING CHARACTERISTIC: ABILITY TO SURVIVE

There is a sorrowful Armenian song that is known by Armenians in both the homeland and the Diaspora. The refrain is a conversation between a Diasporan Armenian far from home and a crane flying overhead. "Do you bring good news from our land?" asks the Diasporan. But the refrain is expressed with such doleful melancholy that everyone knows the answer. The long history of misrule, deportation, and massacre is part of the Armenian experience. Yet, there is another aspect to this song that is uplifting, for Armenians share a sense of having survived it all. Nothing is really shocking and—as history has shown—nothing has knocked them down permanently. Through brutal rulers, war, genocide, earthquakes, and shortages, the Armenian culture has survived. There may not be good news from one's beloved Armenia but, through all the turmoil, there is still a homeland.

Some believe the resilience of the Armenian people is nothing short of a miracle. Others contend it is the Armenian spirit, determination, and, yes, stubbornness, that help them preserve a culture that always gets back on its feet no matter how hard it is knocked down. The first Christian nation, a unique language and alphabet, a relatively homogeneous society—all of these factors must survive as they have for thousands of years. To do everything possible to ensure the culture passes from one generation to the next is to be a true Armenian.

chapter three

FESTIVALS & CUSTOMS

Although weather, economic conditions, and a multitude of other factors can make life harsh in Armenia, very little prevents Armenians from celebrating their holidays. The problems of daily life are forgotten as holiday fever kicks in. And best of all, holidays are often a time for staging huge family events.

Interestingly, the Armenian holiday calendar includes both Christian and pagan festivals. Although many have theorized about why this mix still exists, the simplest explanation is that the early Christians were not known for fun and lively social interactions, whereas the pagans knew how to keep things merry with activities such as jumping over fire and dousing one's friends with buckets of water. Even the major Christian celebrations of Easter and Christmas retain colourful pagan customs from the pre-Christian past.

Of course, for the biggest fanfare, there are the life-event celebrations involving friends and family—baptisms, birthdays, and, most notably, weddings. Attending an Armenian wedding is to see the Armenian family in action. The highs and lows of family life are all there, as the seemingly endless celebration gets under way. It is said that an Armenian wedding is the entire Armenian experience in one momentous event.

THE WINTER HOLIDAYS

The Armenian Church follows the old Julian calendar (devised in 46 BCE), not the reformed Christian calendar introduced by Pope Gregory XIII in 1582. This means that Western visitors may find their usual festivities reversed, as New Year's Day is celebrated before the Armenian Christmas, which is the culmination of the activities of the holiday season.

In recent years, however, the holiday season has started a little earlier, with the additional celebration of Western Christmas on December 25. A large metal tree with the colors of the Armenian flag is now erected in Republic Square by mid-December, and stores often put up their decorations around this time. You will even see a few Santa Clauses waving at crowds in front of stores in downtown Yerevan. On the actual December 25 date, some Armenians get together with family and friends.

New Year's Day

Things really start hopping in the few days before New Year's Day. This is when households prepare for the massive feasts ahead. In the past, these were days of intense food preparation, and it was not uncommon for a household to bake as many as a dozen different types of pastry. However, economic growth has brought more conveniences, and now it is common to see people frantically shopping for food during these preparatory days. You will also see crowded beauty salons as women prepare for the parties ahead. Very wealthy families go to the ski resort Tsakhkadzor, which is almost fully booked for New Year by October.

Some say that the New Year celebrations have also become more lavish. As recently as the 1990s, the Armenian New Year celebration was a quiet family meal at home, followed by local or Russian television as the evening's entertainment. Today, there are not only piles of food, but also gifts—apples and coins for traditionalists and more extravagant items for contemporary families—involved in the celebration. And for some, the New Year means celebratory meals in restaurants.

For those who stick to tradition, there are certain rituals to perform on New Year's Eve. At midnight, lights in the home are extinguished and the family recites the Lord's Prayer together. Then all lights are switched back on and the home is made as bright as possible. Family members partake in a bowl of *anushabour*, a thick, sweet soup made of wheat, sugar, and dried fruit.

New Year's Day is the time to dress up, buy new clothes for the children, and get out the best plates and silverware. Families both contemporary and traditional welcome as many guests as possible to their homes and try to make as many visits to other homes as they can. Some even keep the doors to their houses open during this day to ensure that everyone knows they are welcome.

There's also a flurry of phone calls and SMS messages from well-wishers.

This is definitely not a time to think about one's waistline, as food plays a very big role. On the doorsteps on New Year's Day, you will see purposely broken pomegranates with seeds and pulp lying strewn about the pavement. This is a symbol of hope for abundance in the coming year. Indoors, tables are laden with fruits, grilled meats and fish, candy, and cakes, for guests to  enjoy as they come and go. Armenians believe that the more food there is, and the more guests eating it, the better the year ahead will be.

Christmas

Armenian Christmas is a more sedate celebration with family and, for some, a church service. On Christmas Eve, January 5, traditional families light lanterns and attend church, where the divine liturgy is celebrated and holy communion is received. They bring home a church candle to fill their homes with divine light.

On the morning of January 6, traditional families attend church again. A large basin of water is put in front of the altar, and a cross is submerged in the water to symbolize Christ's baptism. The congregation then approaches the basin and takes some holy water home with them.

For one week following Christmas (until January 13), every day is still considered part of the celebration. Friends and relatives continue to visit each other's homes and greet one another. Some greetings you may hear include, *Tzez yev mes medz avedis* (To everyone, the good news), *Krisdos dzunav yev haydnetsav* (Christ is born and revealed among us), and *Orhnial eh haydnootiunun Krisdosee* (Blessed are the revelations of Christ). On January 13, the holidays, both Diasporan and native Armenian, officially come to an end.

If you are planning any type of business dealings during the holiday period, remember that Armenians take their New Year's and Christmas celebrations seriously. Both January 1 and 6 are state holidays, so businesses are closed. Also, throughout the holiday period, it is almost unheard of not to spend this time with family and friends, so there isn't a lot of business done. However, even if you don't accomplish your business goals, the chances are that you will be invited to someone's home for a great Armenian meal.

IN THE SPRING
St. Sargis Day

St. Sargis Day is celebrated on a Saturday, sixty-three days before Easter. The day is named for St. Sargis, a powerful third-century soldier who rode a white horse and defended Christianity. The day is not a state holiday, but is a favorite with the young and young at heart. According to tradition, you should eat a very salty cake before going to bed and not wash it down with any liquids. Then, you concentrate on your dreams. If you dream about someone pouring a glass of water, that person is destined to be your spouse. Armenians also make a pastry, called *pokhindz*, and leave it in their yards on St. Sargis night. If St. Sargis's horse leaves a hoof print on the pastry, the year ahead will be a good one.

Today, St. Sargis competes with Valentine's Day for the attention of young Armenians. However, since St. Sargis comes first, some modern Armenians see it as a chance to test the affections of their potential love. If the person you're considering appears in your dreams on St. Sargis night, it's definitely worth pursuing that person on Valentine's Day!

Terendez

Another festival, observed the day before Valentine's Day, is Terendez. For the Church, it's the day to celebrate forty days after Jesus' birth. The faithful light candles in church and take the consecrated light back to their homes. However, the real fun of Terendez celebrations comes from the borrowed pagan traditions, for this is a time to "jump the fire." A fire—a pagan symbol of warmth and renewal— is lit, and newly married or engaged couples are encouraged to jump through it to ensure their fertility. In some villages, children and pregnant or new mothers are also invited to make the leap. Afterward everyone is invited to dance, and when the fire is finally extinguished its ashes are distributed among the festival participants. The ash is also considered very important for renewal, and is given to the pregnant and ill to sprinkle on their food or drink. Some people also spread the ash across their fields and cattle sheds, or place it in the stoves they use to make *lavash* (Armenian bread).

What isn't often mentioned in the traditional guides to Armenia is that vodka is also often involved in the Terendez celebration. Ultimately, this can lead to considerable burned shoe leather.

Women's Month
While lovers get their days in February, women get an entire month during the spring. Celebrations begin on Women's Day, March 8, which is a bank holiday. On this day it's traditional to honor the women in your life (wife, mother, aunts, sisters, girlfriend, and even female work colleagues) with gifts such as chocolate and flowers. In Soviet culture, March 8 was dedicated to honor the women's rights movement, but the Armenians have made it more romantic.

Approximately a month later, on April 7, comes Motherhood and Beauty Day. The whole month has become a time for commercial activity. Stores and restaurants offer discounts and promotions, and many nongovernment organizations choose this month to put on special events, lectures, and demonstrations to raise awareness of women's issues.

Genocide Victims' Memorial Day

Every year, on April 24, Armenians honor the memory of the 1.5 million victims of the 1915 genocide (see Chapter 1). In Yerevan, thousands of people join the annual procession from the center of the city to the genocide memorial to pay their respects. Similar processions take place in Diaspora countries across the globe on this day.

Easter

Easter (Zatik) is a favorite day in Armenia. After a cold winter, everyone looks forward eagerly to the holiday. During the Lent period leading up to Easter, Armenian families put lentils or other sprouting grains on a tray, cover them with a cotton cloth, and keep the tray in a light, sunny place in the home. Around Easter time the sprouts will start to appear, symbolizing spring and the world's awakening. The sprouts also become the "grass" for a traditional Armenian centerpiece for the Easter holiday. During Easter you'll also see braided bread and many items, including eggs, painted red to symbolize the blood of Christ.

IN THE SUMMER
Vardavar

If you are doused with a bucket of water on a summer day in Yerevan, don't assume that you are under personal attack! You are now simply another participant in Vardavar, an Armenian holiday occurring on the third Sunday of July.

The custom of pouring water on someone's head on a midsummer day is again rooted in the country's pagan past, when people worshipped Astghik, the goddess of love and beauty. According to legend, Astghik spread love through Armenia by sprinkling rosewater across the land.

Vardavar today is an opportunity for mischievous children, teenagers, and sometimes adults to rattle water buckets and look for somebody to soak. No one is exempt, even those who believe they are protected by being in a car or taxi. Watch out—you may get doused through the window. If you do get splashed, don't be offended.

It's just one day a year, and usually a hot one, so take it as it's meant, in the spirit of good fun.

First Day of the Republic and Independence Day
Technically, Armenia has two Independence Days. The public holiday known as the First Day of the Republic is celebrated on May 28, and marks the formation of the First Armenian Republic in 1918. Although this republic was short-lived, it was significant in that it inspired Armenians with the hope of reestablishing their own nation.

A bigger public holiday is Independence Day, on September 21, the date in 1991 when Armenians overwhelmingly voted to secede from the declining Soviet Union. Two days later, Armenia's first post-Communist parliament formally declared independence.

Since 1991, Independence Day has taken on varied levels of celebration. At first, the country was too preoccupied with war and shortages to do much celebrating. However, in recent years, Armenians have begun marking it with parades, film festivals, concerts, and fireworks displays. As usual on a day off work, people also celebrate with family gatherings.

Other Significant Government Holidays
On May 1, Armenians celebrate **Labor Day** with a public holiday.

On May 9, the Second World War is commemorated with **Victory and Peace Day**. This day was an official holiday throughout the Soviet Union and is still regarded as a significant day in Armenia. Typically, it is a time to remember those who fought in the war.

July 5 is **Constitution Day**, another public holiday. The Constitution of the Republic of Armenia was adopted through a national referendum on July 5, 1995.

On December 7, Armenians honor those who perished in the 1988 earthquake with a **Day of Remembrance**. This is not a public holiday, but it is common to see memorial ceremonies taking place throughout the country on this day.

Fireworks in Yerevan
In the summer, almost every night is marked by a fireworks display in the city center, usually occurring after 10:00 p.m. at the conclusion of the "dancing fountains" at Republic Square. For newcomers, these late-night fireworks commemorating no particular holiday can be a bit disconcerting when one hears loud explosions in the sky, but this is just everyday life in the summer. Be prepared for a very loud display on Independence Day, starting around midnight.

THE WEDDING: THE BIGGEST CELEBRATION OF ALL

A wedding in Armenia is big—often bigger than Christmas and New Year's Day. Wedding celebrations can last several days, and are an opportunity for the entire family—sometimes the entire village—to celebrate in earnest.

When it comes to finding a life mate, Armenians are encouraged to marry not only an Armenian, but a local boy or girl. As the Armenian saying goes, "The best bride is the one who lives on your street." However, the spouse one chooses must not be even remotely related. Tradition dictates that there can be no mixing of bloodlines for as many as seven generations. Given the difficulty of identifying the right potential mate, it is no wonder that Armenians celebrate finding "the right one" with such gusto.

The ritual of matrimony traditionally begins with the proposal. The young man's family is supposed to go to the young woman's house to ask her parents' permission to marry. Everyone engages in a game of "hard to get." The parents—even if they're completely approving of the engagement—are not supposed to agree with the first request. The groom's parents are expected to come back again until the bride-to-be's father relents. And to make the matter that much more difficult, the bride-to-be's father would never say "yes" directly, but he would more typically state, "Let's not argue any more."

Once the engagement is finalized, the wedding plans—and expenses—begin. The costs mount up quickly, not necessarily because of the luxuries involved but because of the hundreds of family members invited. Generally, the groom's family pays for the wedding celebrations, while the bride's family covers the engagement costs—probably a party with a limited guest list. Both families usually give the married couple a special gift. On the wedding day, both the groom's and the bride's houses have parties. Women gather early at the bride's house to help her get dressed. The groom arrives with the dress and shoes (his family has purchased the clothes, but modern brides typically tell him what to buy). Then, someone steals one of the bride's shoes and she is required to pay to get it back. When she has finished dressing, the older women encircle the bride to wish her well.

The church ceremony is relatively short, but filled with ritual. When the bride and groom approach the altar, the priest places crowns on their heads. They then stand forehead to forehead as they receive their blessing. Finally they drink

wine from a shared goblet and are pronounced married. Wedding parties can last for as long as eight or nine hours. Presiding over the wedding and the party is the godfather, chosen by the couple for this position of honor. He not only serves as the leader of the wedding but is expected to offer guidance throughout their married lives. His wife, the godmother, also holds a position of honor and is expected to share her wisdom with them, too.

Wedding guests dance for hours and participate in many, many toasts. A classic one is, "May you grow old on one pillow."

Often the bride is presented with gold jewelry at the party and she dances around the room to show it off. Unmarried friends are given small gifts (*tarosiks*) by the wedding couple as "good luck" tokens, to wish them married soon. It is also believed that if an unmarried person puts their *tarosik* under his or her pillow, the future wife or husband appears in their dreams.

There are several important superstitions surrounding the wedding day. For example, it's a bad sign if two brides see each other on their wedding day. Armenians tend not to get married in May, as this may bring sadness later in life. And the bride and groom are supposed to ward off evil spirits by breaking two decorated plates upon entering their new home. The plates must be broken on the first hit in order for this to be effective.

ARMENIANS AND TRADITION

Of course, in many families, not all celebrations are carried out according to custom, and not all weddings follow all the traditions described above. Old ways are replaced with new ones and modern conveniences offer shortcuts not taken in the past.

However, the maintenance of traditions is a topic of much discussion among families in both Armenia and the Diaspora. Many Armenians feel they must maintain traditions because those families who survived the genocide are obligated to preserve as much of Armenian culture as possible. This heightened sense of awareness is prevalent even among young people, whom the media has exposed to more foreign cultures than any other generation in the past.

Most young people feel privileged to have so many time-honored traditions. Family, culture, and the customs of their past have given them a source of belonging and pride that many of their non-Armenian friends seem to have lost.

chapter four

MAKING FRIENDS

On arrival at the Zvartnots-Yerevan International Airport, you will immediately notice the affection with which Armenians treat their family and friends. Smudged lipstick and massive use of tissues are the order of the day as people arrive or depart. Spend any amount of time in the country and you, too, will experience the warmth of the Armenian people. Eventually you will even hear your name used with the affectionate suffix *jan*, a compliment to you, and a signal that you have made fast friends with your Armenian hosts. *Jan* literally means "body," but it is used much like the Japanese *san*. You may even find yourself using it, in addressing your good Armenian friends.

FRIENDSHIP

Armenians tend to be a warm and open people once you're accepted into the fold. Raised in large extended families, they are used to caring about other people, and know the value of it, and of showing their affection. Other people's children get hugged on the street; colleagues get double-cheek kisses when meeting each other after hours, and almost every acquaintance gets a wave or some other form of greeting on the street. Even the waiter from last night's restaurant may wave at you from the other side of the street.

You should find it fairly easy to get to know people you meet in your daily life. For all its bustling atmosphere, even the capital city of Yerevan is ultimately a small town where everyone seems to know one another. You'll soon find yourself encountering familiar faces in shops and cafés.

Making friends with Armenians is a wonderful thing, as you will probably have acquired friends for life. Armenians are accustomed to staying in close contact with their Diaspora relatives thousands of miles away, so don't be surprised if you regularly hear from your Armenian friends after you return home. They will probably send you e-mails, wanting to know how you and your family are doing. If you can, keep up the correspondence as you will find that maintaining a strong friendship is quite possible, even if your direct contact is limited.

RULES OF ENGAGEMENT

It's important to understand how Armenians conduct their social lives. Most have grown up surrounded by family—not just immediate family but cousins, aunts, and every other member of the bloodline. To be part of this sprawling family tree is most important, so, if you are coming to Armenia as even a distant relative, you have a distinct advantage over the foreigner without Armenian connections. Those with family should be prepared to be spoiled—or even smothered.

If you are coming as a foreigner with no social or familial connections, there are rules of engagement. First, accept Armenians' intense pride for their country. Don't contradict claims of "the best music, the best food, the most beautiful countryside . . ." It's advisable to listen to and appreciate the strong feelings Armenians have for their land. After all, a culture cannot have survived for so long without such strong passions. Second, know that even small gestures go a long way. Armenians are said to have a "second sense" about knowing who is truly genuine. If they regard you as a friendly, well-meaning person, you will quickly gain their friendship.

A Little Pre-Study Goes a Long Way

Armenians in Yerevan are accustomed to having visitors in their homes or businesses, but very often these are relatives or friends from the Diaspora who already know something about their homeland. This basic information includes knowledge of the major towns and cities of the country, famous Armenian artists and writers, and some history of ancient Armenia, the genocide, and modern independence. It's also good to know a few key greetings in the language. This book should help with most of the basics, but it is very beneficial to read some historical texts before coming. A few are listed on page 165.

You will also be expected to have a basic grasp of Armenian names—both first and last. You should be able to correctly pronounce typical names such as Gohar (female, Go-*har*), Gayane (female, Guy-*ahn*-eh), Tigran

(male, Teeg-*ran*-un), Areg (male, A-*reg*), Nane
(female, Na-*neh*), Varduhi (female, Var-du-*hee*),
Arsen (male, Ar-*sen*), Gevorg (male, Gay-*vork*),
and Hasmik (female, Has-*mik*).

Last names often have historical relevance to
the family's occupation or geographical origin.
Showing an appreciation for others' genealogy
will be appreciated.

FIRST MEETINGS

Armenians love to socialize. You'll find
particularly lively parties going on in the cafés,
on the steps of Republic Square, and in the
Vernissage marketplace.

Introducing yourself to a group of Armenians
who are in the midst of socializing would be quite
difficult. You'd probably find yourself trying to
enter a tight clique that has been formed since
school or even birth—they might all be cousins,
or have grown up in the same apartment block.
They aren't likely to stop and translate for a visitor
who doesn't share their past or language.

The best way to start is to invite a new friend or work colleague to join you for tea or a beer. If it's summer, pick an outdoor café. Your friend may be more open to a simple drink than a meal, even if you offer to pay, since restaurant prices are out of reach for many people, whereas sitting at a table and nursing a drink is absolutely acceptable.

If this is a "get to know you" encounter, your Armenian friend will probably engage in some introductory small talk to find out how you like his or her country. A common question is, "How do you like Armenian food?" You may find yourself wondering how to answer this question, especially if you haven't enjoyed a home-cooked Armenian meal yet and have only had the less appealing food available at tourist restaurants. Your best bet is to think of something that you've enjoyed—the fresh fruits, juices, cognac, *lavash*—and rave about it. Armenians don't mind hearing about a few minor issues with their country, but criticizing something as important as the food or culture is ill-advised.

If you must express your reservations about something, the best (and safest) thing to complain about is the traffic in Yerevan. Everyone knows about the aggressive drivers and the risks involved in simply crossing the street. This will also let your friend know that you have a desire to see the city, provided you don't risk life and limb. It can lead to some good sightseeing tips, and perhaps a few pointers about surviving as a pedestrian.

Savvy foreigners let their Armenian friends guide the conversation. They will undoubtedly come up with interesting facts about life in Armenia, both pros and cons, in very little time.

There are several topics that are inadvisable to address, especially if this is an initial encounter. Issues that can become prickly include women and gender roles (although women tend to talk about this more than men), homosexuality, and sexual relations. Observations or inquiries about the Church can be made if done respectfully.

When it comes to politics, there's a sharp divide in society between those pro and those antigovernment. Before making any rash statements in either direction, try to get at least a feel for where the other person stands. Depending on your friend's position, you can be more or less critical about the country's political situation. Most Armenians who are not particularly wealthy will have antigovernment leanings. But antigovernment does not necessarily mean pro-opposition, because people are just as divided about the present opposition in Armenia as they are about the authorities. Many people want change, and dislike the people currently in power, but they aren't fond of the alternatives either.

The chances are that your friends will eventually open up about politics, both local and global, as this is a common topic of conversation. Never interject with comments such as, "I can't believe people don't stand up and protest more about their corrupt politicians," because most Armenians are extremely knowledgeable about world politics. You will get a detailed explanation, in return, of exactly what's corrupt and wrong with your own government!

In exchange for your questions, be prepared to receive several from your Armenian friends.

Armenians tend to be very inquisitive about family backgrounds and personal life, which can sometimes make foreigners feel uneasy. An unmarried woman in her thirties or older will probably be asked why she is single. Although the question doesn't have to be answered, it's best to have a tactful response prepared.

ADDRESSING YOUR FRIENDS

Generally, Armenians prefer to use a person's first name unless addressing someone in authority or much older. As we have seen, the word *jan* is a term of endearment, used after a person's first name. You'll hear this term if you become a close friend.

The big exception to the "first name rule" is when young people address older men and women. Young people are encouraged to show respect for their elders. It is common for children and young adults to refer to older people—even those they do not know—as "auntie," "uncle," "grandmother," or "grandfather."

INVITATIONS HOME

You may arrive in Armenia with a long list of friends of friends or relatives that a Diaspora friend back home has asked you to contact. Don't feel reticent about calling these unknown people: "friends of friends" are warmly welcomed, and by simply dropping a familiar name, you may receive an invitation for tea, or even dinner.

When you are invited into an Armenian home, it is customary to bring a small gift, such as a bottle of wine or candy. A gift from your home country would be welcomed, but it is not necessary. Because the postal service is slow and unreliable, coming

armed with letters, photographs, or gifts from Diaspora relatives is especially appreciated.

When greeting your hosts, a handshake is fine for the first time. However, several air kisses (side-to-side but not skin-to-skin) are expected from those who are more familiar. After the greetings you will be welcomed into the living room and shown to a comfortable seat. If you are invited for a meal, there will be predinner snacks (nuts, salty cookies, and so on) ready on the coffee table, and you will be invited to help yourself. Make sure you take something—no one will eat until you do.

Be prepared to engage in multiple and lengthy toasts before and throughout the meal. As a guest, you will be toasted (say, *Kenats't!* for "Cheers!"). Also, toasts to older relatives are the custom. You should toast your host at some time. But do pace yourself—too many toasts with Armenian cognac or vodka can lead to quick inebriation.

A typical dinner starts with *dolma* (stuffed vine leaves or cabbage leaves), progresses to a meat course, and ends with fruit and dessert. One is usually expected to eat everything on one's plate. And be forewarned—it is customary for the host to replenish a guest's plate quickly once the food is eaten.

WHAT'S IN AN ARMENIAN NAME?

You will know that Armenian family names tend to end with —ian or, more commonly in post-Soviet Armenia, with —yan. In Turkey, you will find the —ian replaced by —oglu. In Russia, many change to —ov endings, as in Gary Kasparov, or —ski, like Aivazyan-Aivazovski, a famous Armenian–Russian painter. But this is just one part of the story. A family name can indicate geographic origin, occupation, aristocracy, or other trait.

Names beginning with a first name and ending with —ian or —yan are indications of the father's first name. Diasporans tend to use —ian, while Armenians use —yan. For example, Davidian is the son of David, and Krikorian is the son of Krikor or Gregor. Typically, first names were taken from the Bible, so many last names have a religious origin. (Sokhomonyan is the son of Solomon.)

Some last names are based on the name of the place the family originally came from. For example, the last name of Vanetzian comes from the word Vanetzi, a person who was born in Van. Another example is Sasunyan, someone who came from Sasun.

An ending of —uni or —ooni may indicate that the family is from the ancient Armenian aristocracy of Parthian Persia (the Nakharar class). Not many of these names survive today. Examples are Sasuni and Rshtuni.

Interestingly, names that indicate the occupation of an ancestor were often given by tax collectors, who had to identify people for tax purposes. Since the collectors might have been Turks, Persians, or Arabs, the names often have their roots in languages other than Armenian, and can differ significantly between eastern and western Armenians, as the eastern names often have their roots in Persian, Georgian, or Russian, while the western ones may have theirs in Turkish, Arabic, or Greek. The names Najarian, Darbinyan, Koshkaryan, and Derzakyan mean, respectively, the son of a carpenter, blacksmith, shoemaker, and tailor.

The oddest names are those based on a distinguishing trait of an ancestor. For example, Harutunian means "son of the resurrection"—the first owner of the name was probably born around Easter.

Names with the prefix Der or Ter indicate that an ancestor was a Der Hayr, a married parish priest, a position of great social standing in Armenia. Two common examples are Der Bedrosian and Ter Petrosian.

Many Diasporan names are shortened or modified, and often drop the —ian ending. For example, Mugerditchian or Mkrtichian became Mugar, and Sargasyan became Sark.

(*Adapted from a study of Armenian names by Gary Lind-Sinanian of the Armenian Library and Museum of America in Massachusetts.*)

DATING

The uncertainty of "is this really a date?" barely exists in Armenia. It is highly unusual for young people to be just friends with the opposite sex, so if you invite someone (or are invited) just for a drink, it does indeed count as a date. At the very least, it is a strong indication that the other person is interested in you romantically. Also be warned that if you are a Western foreigner, you will be seen as more sexually available than a native Armenian. It is possible that "a beer is just a beer," but it may also be perceived as a prelude to something more.

When it comes to family, your Armenian dating partner will probably not take you home to meet the parents unless it is a very serious relationship. While there is plenty of dating that goes on without parents knowing about it, the older generation tends to believe you should only date the person you are going to marry, so casual partnering would be completely perplexing to—or even forbidden by—many parents. Casual dating in rural Armenia is almost unheard of unless marriage is the clear end. However, even in Yerevan, dating someone for longer than a year or eighteen months without marrying or at the very least getting engaged is also highly unusual.

Dating foreigners is usually just for women. Although some Armenian men will date foreign women, they tend to look for Armenian brides. There are many reasons for this, but the most likely is that an Armenian wife will be more inclined to keep a traditional Armenian household.

In dating, as in friendships, know that there will be cultural differences. Never assert that your customs are superior, and always remain open to new ways of doing things. Whether you find the love of your life or simply gain new friendships, getting to know the people of Armenia can be a life-enhancing experience.

chapter five

THE ARMENIANS AT HOME

THE ARMENIAN HOME

The high cost of housing in Yerevan has kept many Armenians living in older buildings. Some of these are in the charming "Tamanian" style. In the 1920s, the architect Alexander Tamanian planned the city of Yerevan and introduced many classically designed buildings to the city, decorating them with intricate stone carvings and ornamentation. Tamanian built with tuf, a distinctly strong, pink stone of volcanic rock (thus giving Yerevan the title of "the pink city"). Living in a Tamanian building is a source of pride.

However, most families in the city tend to live in the large Soviet concrete apartment buildings that went up during the latter half of the twentieth century. From the outside, they look like formidable monstrosities that are about to crumble at a moment's notice. Once you are inside, however, you will probably find something much more pleasant. With most families choosing to remodel rather than move, the interiors of these old concrete apartment complexes can be quite luxurious. Don't be surprised to find heated wooden floors, spacious, well-furnished living rooms for receiving guests, and modern kitchens with dishwashers.

On the sloping hills just outside Yerevan, you may see housing developments of lavish, multistory mansions, resembling the American "McMansions" that populate the wealthiest suburbs of the USA. These are the well-appointed homes of Armenia's few wealthy families, usually of the oligarchy.

In contrast, life in an Armenian village is very different. Houses are built of stone or inexpensive materials. Although some homes have been improved, the majority of people live quite poorly, and for some, heating and plumbing are luxuries still out of reach.

Owning Property in Armenia

Although borrowing from a bank to buy a house is a relatively new idea in a country accustomed to the tradition of state-provided housing, more and more young couples are embarking on mortgages for home ownership. Not only is this seen as a change from the traditional multigenerational living arrangements (see below), but it is also a sign that there is a new generation interested in getting credit to finance their futures.

To meet the demand for more home loans, some banks have been changing their lending policies. Typically, they asked for a 25 or 30 percent down payment, with ten-year mortgages and interest rates in the high teens. Now, lenders are offering lower down payments and longer payoff periods, although foreigners might still consider the terms somewhat limiting.

Of course, the price of a new apartment or house has become prohibitive for some young people; but there are signs that more changes are ahead. Presenting his vision of Armenia in five years' time, the country's prime minister has pledged, "Any newly created family will have an opportunity to buy an apartment and a car."

FAMILY STRUCTURE

Traditionally, the newly married couple's first home is with the husband's family. For the young wife this can sometimes be a serious power struggle. The senior woman acts as head of the household, managing daily life and overseeing household chores. These are carried out by the youngest female(s) in the family unit, thus the new bride (*hars*) is expected to serve not only her husband but the entire family, doing everything from food preparation to laundry, perhaps alongside her sisters-in-law if they are still at home. (It should be emphasized that while this still takes place in more old-fashioned families, modern families wouldn't expect this.) Eventually, the young couple will save enough money to move out, but this usually means going to live just down the street from the family.

In rural areas, families tend to be quite large. There is a government stipend for families with three or more children, but this is a relatively small amount of money and would not usually justify having an exceptionally large family. In Yerevan, families are smaller. Abortions are legal, and tend to be the preferred, affordable form of birth control (oral contraceptives are available but expensive). Several women's groups are currently examining family size and reproductive services in Armenia from a social and economic perspective.

Although birthrates have declined, Armenia is a relatively young country. Young people clearly outnumber retirees on the streets of Yerevan, their presence radiating an energy that is palpable in the city. One gets the sense that these young people will have a lot to say about the future of their families and their country.

GROWING UP IN ARMENIA

The education system is undergoing changes in Armenia. For years, the country followed the Soviet system, with primary education starting at the age of seven. However, the Ministry of Education is changing from the Soviet style of ten to eleven years of primary and secondary schooling to the Western system of twelve years. Therefore, children will be required to start school at the age of five. The intention is to give more time to the arts and nontraditional subjects that were not provided in years past. Also, children start going to school on Saturdays in fourth grade.

Yerevan State University is the largest university in Armenia. Founded in 1919, it has 110 academic departments with approximately 1,350 postgraduate students and

8,500 undergraduates. If you are anywhere near the university at practically any time of day, it appears that the whole world is composed of twenty-year-old college students.

Other universities include the Russian-Armenian State University, Université Française en Arménie, and the American University Armenia, all in Yerevan. Much newer than Yerevan State, all of these are also gaining reputations as solid educational institutions.

EVERYDAY SHOPPING

Armenians spend a lot of time shopping and, given all the options, it's understandable. Yerevan shoppers can buy their food and other goods in a range of outlets from modern supermarkets to street vendors. The secret is to know which items to buy in which venue.

The big supermarkets are mostly chains, located throughout the city. Although prices tend to be much higher than the "mom and pop" grocers, the selection is far greater. Crowds gather right before the dinner hour, with working women rushing about buying the ingredients of the evening meal. Since most of the big markets are open day and night, it's best to time one's visits outside peak hours, when the service is better and shelves more fully stocked. A phenomenon of some self-service stores in Armenia is the "retail hoverers" who shadow you up and down the aisles. Although they are there to help you find what you want, their presence can be distracting for those more accustomed to shopping without assistance.

For small purchases, there is a mom-and-pop grocery store on every street. The choice is not great in these shops, and it's almost never "self-serve." You must tell the woman—it's nearly always a woman—behind the counter exactly what you are looking for. Foreigners may point if necessary. There is usually a woman assigned to each specific area of the store—the bread, the cheese, the cleaning products, and so on. She won't help you with an item outside her area; if you've got your bread and you want cheese, you have to wait for the cheese woman to be available.

As for fresh produce, Armenians don't purchase this in the stores—either the mom and pops or, especially, the supermarkets. The choice in these places is usually not particularly varied, and they often wrap their day-old items in plastic and sell it in larger quantities. When you get it home you may find that the better-looking produce is arranged on the top of the pack, with older, perhaps unusable, fare underneath it. In other words, you haven't got a bargain.

Yerevan housewives know that the best deal in town for fruit and vegetables will be found with the street vendors, whose produce is usually freshly picked and significantly less expensive than what is available in stores. In the warmer months, they sell many mouthwatering varieties of fruits and vegetables. You will find these

vendors on the street or in small pockets of the city, such as the communal area for the apartment block behind Sakharov Square.

For the biggest variety of produce, try the large open-air markets known as *shukas*. These are busy places, and you should allow yourself plenty of time to shop here. *Shukas* are stocked with freshly butchered meat (sometimes set apart from the main *shuka*), fish (both freshly killed and live), fruit and vegetables, spices, dairy products, breads, and some prepackaged goods. Sellers in the *shuka* will usually offer you a taste before you buy. One of the best times to shop there is in the fall, when the apples and grapes are in season and there are vast displays of dried fruits. It's quite easy to fill up on free samples before ever deciding on your purchase!

There are no fixed prices in the *shuka*, so bargaining is usually expected. Foreigners are often told that almost everything is 1,000 drams —it isn't. The best phrase to learn is *verchin gina inch eh?* (vehr-*cheen* geen-ah eench eh?), which means "What's the final price?" Often, though, you will find farmers outside the entrances offering the same quality items more cheaply.

Baked goods are somewhat of a luxury for Armenians on a tight budget, but there are several good bakeries throughout Yerevan. The savviest shoppers know exactly when the cakes are made, and therefore when they can buy the products at their freshest. There are plenty of familiar-looking chocolate and vanilla cakes on display, but do try the traditional walnut and honey treats and the national dessert, a sweet bread called *gata*.

The Vernissage

For more than thirty years shoppers have flocked to the open-air market known as the Vernissage. Much more than just an interesting tourist attraction, this is the place where Yerevan residents can now purchase everything from oil paintings to showerheads.

Originally, this market was a place where local artists could show their work to the general public—the French word *vernissage* (varnishing) is used to mean a private display held before the opening of an art exhibition. However, when crowds gathered to view the paintings, local merchants saw an opportunity to sell their own wares. They began bringing their products to the area and the outdoor space became a "super market" selling a wide variety of items.

Although some Vernissage vendors are there throughout the week, the real action is on weekends. The main market starts by the Republic

Square metro station and runs all the way to Khanjian Street, progressing from the vendors of everyday items (plumbing supplies, remote controls, tools both new and used) to artwork, embroidered rugs, and jewelry, as one travels away from the Republic Square side. Perhaps the oddest displays of goods are those on the margins of the market, where one finds chemicals, beakers, microscopes, test tubes, forceps, and other surgical supplies. There are few actual buyers for these.

For the Yerevanite, going to the Vernissage means picking up some needed household items or looking through the vast collection of books. For tourists, it's a chance to sample local color and purchase souvenirs and gifts.

It is perfectly appropriate to bargain at the Vernissage. Many of the sellers speak English or Russian. However, merchants can quickly assess who's local and who's a tourist, and, naturally, tourists pay more.

THE WORKING DAY

The day begins early in Yerevan. If you live by the Cascade, you'll be woken up by the sound of the wild dogs on the hill. Anywhere else, you'll hear the noise of traffic, bright and early. The main rush starts around 8:00 a.m., with commuters hurrying to work on foot, or via the metro or *marshrutka*. Children are going to school, accompanied by their mothers in high heels, who then dash off to work. The Armenian woman's ability to run in high heels is legendary, and particularly impressive is her skill in negotiating the many staircases of Yerevan without falling. Shops usually open around 9:00 a.m., when you'll see women sweeping the sidewalks.

After the morning rush, the pace slows in the city. It picks up again around 5:00 or 6:00 p.m., when families hurry home for dinner.

WORK LIFE

Perhaps the biggest challenge of work life in Armenia is to find a job with livable wages. Unfortunately, businesses coming to Armenia often think that it's a developing nation where people aren't looking for salaries on the Western scale. Nothing could be farther than the truth, however. With the cost of living climbing significantly, Armenians want—and need— equitable wages. Some address the shortfall in salaries by taking on two or even three jobs. Others take low-paid work to tide them over until something better comes along, which is frustrating for their employers. And there are those who look for work outside the country.

These days, many of the available jobs are in the civil service. Many university students aspire to government positions, which are often considered the best available. Although obtaining these jobs is often difficult, those who do are regarded as very successful and as making a contribution to their country.

Other young people (primarily the university graduates) find employment with the many international nongovernmental organizations working on grants and relief efforts throughout the country, such as WorldVision, the World Wildlife Foundation, and UNICEF. These tend to pay low but steady wages, and offer valuable work experience. Many such organizations have names that are recognizable to global employers and look useful on a résumé.

Most young people who secure good jobs will put their heart into their working life. They run on tight schedules and don't take time out for leisurely lunches. It is not unusual to see young men and women working late into the night to finish a project or assignment and, even after hours away from the workplace, making and receiving business calls on their cell phones.

While young people are very aware of the need to find a good job and have a career, older Armenians still hark back to the Soviet life when there were jobs available for almost everyone. Those first to get on the subway after work are almost invariably the mid to older age group who easily separate job from family obligations. For them, getting home to the family for supper is most important.

As the "baby boomers" of Armenia start to retire, they are also concerned that they will not be as well protected as their parents are in their old age. In Armenia, pensions are typically 20,000 drams per month, or about US $65—hardly enough even to buy groceries.

In the rural areas, the economy is much bleaker. The most fortunate are hired for government jobs. Others rely on small-scale agriculture. For young people, the answer is almost always to go to Yerevan to look for work.

MILITARY SERVICE

Although intensely patriotic, the Armenian public is somewhat divided on its attitude toward military conscription— perhaps a hangover from Soviet times when Armenians held large demonstrations against the draft that often took soldiers to all parts of the Soviet Union. This attitude continued in the post-Soviet period. In the first two years of independence, recruitment fell far short of quotas.

Today, young men between the ages of eighteen and twenty-six must give two years of military service. The exceptions are those enrolled in

state-run universities, a situation which has resulted in many young men staying in graduate school until their twenty-seventh birthday, when they cease to be eligible. However, there is talk of abolishing this exemption as the country attempts to draft young men born in the early 1990s—a period of sharp decline in the birthrate and massive emigration.

Those opposed to lifting the exemption for university students believe that appealing to national pride should be enough. They contend that young people already have a fierce pride in their country and that simply appealing to this should fill the ranks with recruits.

TIME OUT

GETTING AWAY FROM IT ALL

Traditionally, Yerevan's wealthier residents
summered in the mountains or at Lake Sevan,
where guesthouses and summer homes provided
relief from the sweltering city. Beaches filled up
with sunbathers, and in the evening the heady
scent of barbecue was everywhere. But now the
price of vacations even within Armenia has risen
beyond the reach of most people. A reservation in
a guesthouse in the resort town of Jermuk costs
close to the average person's monthly salary, and
skiing trips during the winter have become almost
exclusively for the very rich.

For those lucky enough to have the funds for a vacation away, the options are changing. Some people have found cheaper possibilities in neighboring countries. The Armenian Tourism Development Foundation reports that travel to Georgia has almost doubled over the past several years. Recently, a special train service was started from Yerevan to Batumi and travel agents began offering "special deals" just for Armenians who need their drams to go farther. Another location of growing interest is Turkey. Although the borders are still closed, recent relaxing of restrictions has increased the popularity of the Turkish Mediterranean coast, particularly Antalya. Armenian families are attracted by the relatively low cost and high quality of services there, as well as the availability of cheap, chartered flights from Zvartnots Airport, which are also easing their apprehensions about crossing the border. Bulgaria has become another relatively inexpensive travel choice. And, for the far wealthier, access to Dubai and Athens is relatively easy from Zvartnots.

OUT AND ABOUT

While expensive vacations to far-off lands are still a distant dream for most Armenians, they don't feel they have to work all the time. Even ambitious white-collar professionals with constantly ringing cell phones know to power down occasionally.

Armenians value their leisure moments as an opportunity to socialize, and, as we have seen, time off usually means time spent with family or friends: there are plenty of family dinners and special events to celebrate, such as birthdays and anniversaries. At other times it can just mean enjoying a trip to the park.

Going out to a film or concert with friends is a great way to unwind. And with Yerevan's recent revival of film and other arts, there are plenty of good options. The most popular places to meet, however, are the cafés and bars. After work and well into the night, café tables are usually filled with young people talking, laughing, and, of course, smoking. While older men tend to huddle over a backgammon board, the café has become the new place for the younger generation. As for bars, they're full of the young adults who are part of Yerevan's new set of "beautiful people."

Looking Good

Who says looks aren't everything? They obviously haven't been to a Yerevan bar or disco!

Despite their small incomes, Armenians are very eager to dress up and look good. In fact, many young adults find it incomprehensible that many foreigners dress so untidily. In Yerevan you can easily tell the local from the foreigner by what they are wearing—no self-respecting Armenian would be seen in shorts, tattered jeans, tennis shoes, or sloppy sandals. And cropped blouses, short shorts, plunging necklines, and other revealing clothes that are popular with many female visitors are never worn by Armenian women of any generation.

Armenian women in particular take pride in looking their best. With their perfect olive complexions and shining dark hair, they simply will not be outdone. Hair is usually long and well trimmed, nails are perfectly manicured, and clothes bear the labels (either real or  knockoff) of top designers. Shoes are nearly always high heels for the younger crowd, even during the snow and ice of winter, and how women remain standing in heels during bad weather is often remarked on. Businesswomen wear sharply tailored suits.

With all this emphasis on dressing up, shopping for clothes and accessories is becoming a national sport. There are several "big name" labels, such as Armani, with retail operations in the smart area of North Avenue, but the cost of these clothes is considerably out of reach for the typical Yerevanite. Instead, there are fashion label knockoffs readily available, and less expensive stores in the shopping malls, though you should prepare for some sticker shock. With few items made in Armenia, clothes are generally imported from the West and very expensive. Sometimes the quality of the fabrics is also disappointing given the price tag. To keep their closets varied and within budget, many Armenian women trade clothes with friends or relatives, and they will find several creative ways to wear one particularly dashing item of clothing.

As for jewelry, large silver necklaces with semiprecious stones (onyx, amber, opal, and malachite) are currently popular, and dangling earrings typically adorn Armenian ears. In the open-air markets, such as the Vernissage, it's easy to find jewelry with traditional designs such as the "evil eye," as well as modern styles. Don't be afraid to do as the locals do and bargain with the vendors for a better deal.

Going to the hairdresser is another important activity, and you can find salons on practically every street in Yerevan, where as well as having your hair done you can have a manicure, pedicure, or facial. The practitioners are quite skilled, and salons work hard to ensure that patrons feel pampered. These services are also relatively inexpensive and there are usually "tiered" prices for various levels of treatment and the different product brands (this is especially true of hair colors, where patrons are asked which brand they prefer). Don't worry, blondes and redheads: Yerevan hairdressers know how to achieve just the right shade!

Men also dress sharply, typically wearing dark clothes and black leather shoes. Suits are *de rigueur* for businessmen, usually accompanied by ties. Colors are kept subtle, if added at all. Loud tones such as bright blue and pink are not usually worn, or appear only as accent pieces. Hair is kept short, and most young men pay careful attention to the latest styles. Long hair and ponytails are extremely uncommon and primarily seen on expatriates or artists who want to rebel from the mainstream.

Interestingly, with all the emphasis on looking good, gyms are not as popular as they are in Western countries. Some of the "big name" Western-style gyms are coming to Yerevan, but membership is expensive and the very large gyms are located away from the city center. Some hotels with gyms allow local residents to sign up for membership. The facilities are usually small but well equipped with the usual exercise machines, and many have indoor pools as well. Or, there is the practical alternative. Most women in Yerevan remain slim by walking long distances throughout the city and staying incredibly busy all the time!

CAFÉ LIFE

So what's all the fuss about Yerevan's legendary cafés? The sheer number of them should be indicative of just how popular these places have become. Indeed, ask anyone what people do in Yerevan during the summer, and the response will usually be "go to an outdoor café." Café life is integral to Yerevan culture, and in this respect, visitors are often reminded of the Middle East. During the summer the cafés are crowded with young people meeting for a drink or coffee. Music is often loud, and cigarette smoke is abundant (there are very few nonsmoking establishments in Yerevan).

Cafés are usually situated in the parks, especially by Opera Square—somewhat controversially, as this was formerly an open green space. Abovian Street is another popular café spot, although it offers little greenery. Many cafés open around 11:00 a.m. and stay busy until after midnight. Some have outdoor couches and comfortable chairs and resemble a well-furnished living room. A few offer live music, and there is the ubiquitous "Eurobeat" to accompany your meal.

Of course, the outdoor cafés are seasonal, but the proprietors will try to stretch their business season for as long as possible. Most establishments open in the spring and remain in business until mid-October before closing down for the winter.

RESTAURANTS

Armenians are very proud of their national fare, and restaurants with traditional Armenian food abound. Be sure to ask a local for the best

Armenian restaurants, which are usually not for the tourist trade. There, you will delight in the delicious traditional fare that includes tempting appetizers, wonderful soups, and barbecued meats. Steer clear of the tourist restaurants that advertise (usually in English) "traditional Armenian food." These establishments should really be labeled "traditional bland post-Soviet fare." There you will find mysterious salads, day-old bread, and tough, tasteless chicken and beef. If you want an excellent, low-cost, barbecue, try the restaurants on Proshian Street, known as Barbecue Street. Also, Yerevan is a good place to find Mediterranean food. *Shwarma* is very popular, as are hummus, kebabs, and pita bread.

Be warned that there are very few indoor restaurants with nonsmoking areas (65 percent of the Armenian male population smoke). In the winter this can be a bit unappealing, as the smoke levels are high, and then there is something to be said for the outdoor food stands, even during the colder weather.

In most restaurants, you wait until someone offers to show you to a table. You can ask to see a menu before you are seated. It's likely that someone will speak English, and that there'll be an English or multi-language menu available. Restaurant prices are usually reasonable when compared to their American or British counterparts, but note that in some places (especially outdoor cafés) you may be charged more for sitting in special areas of the restaurant.

Late at night, many nightclubs provide a full menu and are good places to eat after midnight, when most restaurants are already closed. Sometimes, you'll get a singing or dancing show along with your meal. You can also order an expensive, exotic drink and, of course, you can smoke. Some restaurants and clubs also offer a hookah.

If possible, try to get out to the countryside, where there are many outstanding fish and barbecue restaurants in lovely rustic settings. Diners sit in small, private cabins, where they are served with expertly prepared fish and meats and fresh fruit and vegetables. It will remind you of all the natural splendor and serenity of summer camp, but with much better food! Traveling further outside the city, restaurants around the resort towns near Lake Sevan are known for barbecued fish dishes, and in Dilijan for the oyster mushroom dishes. Armenians call the large scenic outdoor restaurants *veteroks* (Russian for "breeze"). As with any popular tourist destination, look for where the local people go, rather than where the large tourist buses stop. You'll get a better meal at more reasonable prices.

Although most restaurants tend to lean toward Armenian food, you can find virtually any international-style restaurant in Yerevan. For example, there are Mexican, Indian, Japanese, and Chinese restaurants all located within a block or two of the Opera House, and Tibetan and Arabic places within walking distance of Republic Square. To account for local taste, most also offer traditional Armenian food.

When you have finished eating, don't expect anyone to rush you out of your seat, as they do in an American restaurant. You will have to ask for the bill before anyone will bring it to you. Although cash is still king, those restaurants accepting credit cards usually accept Visa or MasterCard (Diners Club and American Express are rarely accepted).

TIPPING

Tipping usually starts from the time you arrive at the airport. If someone offers to carry your luggage, it's an indication that they will expect a tip. Your taxi driver from the airport will also expect a tip; about 10 to 15 percent is the rule. In restaurants, again reckon 10 to 15 percent. And yes, as a foreigner, you are expected to tip often and tip well.

THE ARMENIAN PLATE

Armenian food is highly symbolic of the country's shared experience. It reflects the bounty of the countryside, the peoples' love for ancient traditions, respect for religious practices, and the influences from outside that have been part of the country's long and varied history.

Unique to Armenia is that many foods remain pure Hayastan, no matter what political force is in power at the time. Typically Armenian dishes include pumpkin stew (*ghapama*), yogurt soup (*tahnabour*), Armenian meatballs (*Hayastan kiufta*), Sevan trout (*ishkan*), lamb porridge (*harisse*), and boiled soup from cow's hooves (*khash*—more about this later).

At their best, Armenian dishes are made with fresh produce grown in the country's temperate and abundant valleys. Figs, apricots, apples, persimmons, cherries, pomegranates, oranges, and grapes are common ingredients in traditional

Why So Many Pomegranates?

The enigmatic *noor*, or pomegranate, holds a special place in Armenian culture as symbolic of the cycle of life and renewal. According to legend, each one of the translucent red seeds represents a day in this year of your life (a whole is believed to contain 365). If you eat a seed a day, it is said to bring you good luck! Pomegranates are also red, a color revered by Armenians. It represents all the blood that has been shed over centuries for the sake of Hayastan.

Pomegranates are a healthy choice. The fruit is very high in vitamins C and B, and there are claims that it includes antioxidants. However, eating them takes a special skill and some patience. You open the fruit by scoring it with a knife and breaking it open so that the arils (seed casings) are separated from the peel and internal white pulp membranes. There are those who insist on eating the entire seed with the casings, although the watery aril is the most delicious part. The less adventurous can purchase plenty of pomegranate juice in Armenian markets.

The Armenian director Sergei Parajanov released the film *The Color of Pomegranates* in 1968. It was praised by critics and won many prestigious awards, but it was ultimately censored and banned in the Soviet Union for being too avant-garde. It is a biography of the Armenian poet Sayat Nova that depicts his life through dreamlike images from Parajanov's imagination and the author's poems. The lead actor plays six roles, both male and female, and there is little dialogue or camera movement. However, it is considered a landmark film of the Armenian cinematic movement.

dishes. Tomatoes, cucumbers, arugula, leeks, and sweet corn are also typically incorporated into meals.

There is a certain pride in the fact that an Armenian meal takes time to make. Some recipes go back a thousand years or more and are very demanding in their preparation. Many traditional Armenian cooks would rather spend this time on preparation than adjust the recipes by resorting to modern conveniences. The fruit mixture for *bastegh* (similar to a fruit roll-up) requires ten days to dry. *Soujouk* (a beef jerky), usually made in the early fall, takes two days to prepare and another month before it is ready to eat.

Religion and community also play key roles in preparation. For example, there is *madagh,* an Armenian commemoration of the genocide, which involves religious services and large gatherings of people to share a communal meal. Typical foods for *madagh* include lamb stew with pilaf made from bulgur, and *lavash* (see below). The food takes days to prepare, and many individuals in the community help out.

Some say that Armenian food is Middle Eastern, but this is only partly true. Armenian cuisine is heavily influenced by the Middle East, but European and Mediterranean cultures have also shaped its history. You can find *baba ganoush, tabouleh, hummus,* and *halvah* on many Armenian tables, but you can also find pizza and French fries.

Lavash

The staple of nearly every meal is *lavash,* a soft, thin, flat bread made with flour, water, and salt. Almost every restaurant serves it, and almost

anything can ultimately get rolled up into it and eaten as a meal. Armenian *lavash* is very different from and much thinner than what is sold in Western countries.

As with many Armenian foods, lavash takes a lot of time and effort to prepare. It is almost always made by hand. The dough is rolled out flat and cooked against the hot walls of a traditional *lavash* oven (similar to a *tandoor* oven). The length of the *lavash* must be between twenty-four and twenty-eight inches and the width twelve to fifteen inches. It must not be thicker than a twelfth of an inch. Because *lavash* is such a revered staple of Armenian life, some bakers form a cross in the dough before it is baked—a small homage to God for providing this basic necessity.

While flexible like a tortilla when fresh, *lavash* dries out quickly and becomes brittle and hard after a few hours. A small amount of water can bring it temporarily back to life, but it is nearly impossible to store overnight and should not be put in the refrigerator—it will just be dry crumbs in the morning.

Khash and Khashing

One Armenian food tradition that remains inscrutable to most Westerners is the *khash* party. Bluntly, it is a festival of soup that is made with tripe and hooves. But of course, like most traditions, it is much more than that.

Khashing is an antidote to the long Armenian winters. While not everyone can afford to go skiing or travel to warmer climates, almost anyone can go khashing and have a really good time (whether they actually eat the soup or not). In an Armenian village a *khash* party can go on for days.

Many Middle Eastern cultures have dishes similar to *khash*. In the old days, the poorest people had to make do with scraps of meat discarded by the wealthy. So, from necessity, the villagers concocted dishes to make the fare as edible as possible. Making *khash* is an extremely labor-intensive process. First, the meat must be cleaned, soaked, and exfoliated—a process that

can take more than twenty-four hours. Then, when the soup is cooking, one must stand over the pot and skim it at regular intervals. And there must be constant checking to see if it has reached the proper sticky consistency.

Once it is ready, *khash* is served with garlic, parsley, radishes, and *lavash*. *Kash-lavash* is a rhyme you'll frequently hear at a *khash* get-together. The *lavash* can either go right into the soup or be used to pull apart the sticky *khash*. Another ingredient to khashing that is not to be missed is, of course, vodka, which is very much a part of the social ritual.

If you are invited to a *khash* party, you simply must go. And don't worry—most first timers are forgiven if they don't completely empty their bowls.

Breakfast (*Nakhadjash*) and Lunch (*Djash*)

Armenians have the knack of eating well. Although supper is the main meal, there are plenty of opportunities to taste Armenian specialties throughout the day.

For breakfast, most Armenians on the run have strong coffee, perhaps with pastries or bread and jam. In restaurants you can usually get a more substantial meal that includes cold meats, fish, pickled vegetables, and omelets. An omelet of whipped eggs and fresh tomatoes is also fairly traditional, and you can usually order this in a hotel too. In rural Armenia, people enjoy fresh mountain yogurt (*matsun*) that comes in several consistencies. Sometimes honey or sugar is added to sweeten it.

Traditionally, midday meals are light. Salads, potatoes, and breaded or barbecued meats are often available in restaurants. Pizzas have also become popular in Yerevan. Some establishments will offer smaller portions for the lunchtime crowd. On warm days it's typical to pick up a *shwarma* or other quick lunch at an outdoor food stand (usually standing room only).

The Main Event: Dinner (*En-triq*)
The evening meal occurs sometime after 5:00 p.m.
Most families eat a couple of hours later, when
work, school, and shopping are completed and
the mother has had time to prepare the meal.
Restaurants and cafés typically serve dinner late,
sometimes up to midnight.

Most families do not indulge in a full-scale
Armenian meal every night, so it is a special treat
to participate in one. If you do get an invitation to
go to a house where dinner will be served for
guests, it will be an experience that you—and
your stomach—will not forget.

When you arrive, there are usually some
delicious appetizers put out in the living room. Be
careful with these, as it is quite possible to eat so
much that you will have no room for the rest of
the meal. Typically, appetizers feature Armenian
cheese, sliced sausage, hummus, bean and
vegetable salads, and bread. *Dolmas* are also
popular, made with vine leaves in the summer
and cabbage in the winter. There's always *lavash* at
this stage too.

The first course is usually soup (such as *spas*,
made of yogurt and wheat, or *borscht*) or another
specialty dish such as a cheese turnover or spiced
meat. Thankfully, these are usually served in small
portions, as there is plenty yet to come.

The main course is a variation on meat or fish,
and in some cases both. The health conscious will
be glad to note that meats, vegetables, and fish are
often steamed, grilled, or barbecued. The Arab-
inspired *shashlick* (a Russian word), which is
called *khorovats* in Armenian, is grilled, and not

necessarily served on a skewer. Also popular is *baskyrtat*, which are extremely thin strips—almost threads—of boiled beef mixed with walnuts and

cilantro (coriander) and covered with yogurt. Most main-course dishes are served with rice.

Fruit and dessert usually complete the menu, along with a cup of strong Armenian coffee. Western-style cakes and pastries can also make an appearance, although you may have some sticky *baklava* to end the meal.

Armenians do believe in the "clean plate club," so take everything slowly and try to finish whatever you are served. And do not be surprised if you find that once you clean your plate, your host puts even more on it. When you have had enough, you can say, *shat merci, kust em,* or *shnorhakalutjun, kust em* (thanks, I'm full), or *el che* (no more), or *bavarar e* (that's enough!")

A Late Snack

For those still in the mood for food before retiring, there's always the late-night snack. This may consist of herbal or British tea, bread and jam, and sometimes yogurt. A specialty of Armenia is *popoki muraba* (walnut preserve), which is made from green walnuts boiled in sweet syrup until very tender. It is a uniquely Armenian dish, and often available in the countryside.

TO DRINK

Children—and many adults too—delight in Armenia's wide variety of fresh fruit juices. Flavors such as banana and black cherry are available in stores and most restaurants. Tea is not as popular as coffee, which is usually served strong. Mineral waters from the countryside are in abundance, and are a source of pride. Bottled water is a fairly new phenomenon which came about as foreign visitors (especially Americans) began asking for it.

The national alcoholic beverage is cognac. In fact, Armenian cognac was a favorite of Winston Churchill (who eagerly awaited his shipment of Armenian cognac after Stalin introduced him to it at Yalta). The famed Ararat cognac comes from the Ararat Valley, where the volcanic soil lends itself well to growing cognac grapes.

Varieties of cognac are graded by age—the best is usually more than twelve years old. You can tour several cognac manufacturers in Yerevan. Armenian mulberry vodka, which is both manufactured and made in Armenian homes, is very popular. Besides being tasty, it is believed to have some curative qualities.

Wines have had a more checkered history than cognac. Armenians had a three-thousand-year history of winemaking, but after the fall of the Soviet Union the Russian market for wine dried up, large vineyards closed, and the quality and quantity of production deteriorated. Although wine producers are trying to make a comeback, they are now competing with inexpensive wines from Australia, Argentina, Chile, and Georgia. The Armenian red wines that are currently produced tend to be far superior to the whites.

CULTURAL EVENTS

It is not all cafés and eating in Armenia. Time out is also devoted to music, the visual arts, theater, and film. In Yerevan, one can sense a clear revival and new appreciation for Armenian arts. Galleries, concert venues, and theaters are thriving throughout the city.

Film

Much of this excitement is about Armenian films. Ask any local devotee, and he or she will enthusiastically tell you that the film industry in Armenia is taking off. A new, talented generation of filmmakers is clearly focused on telling the Armenian story in innovative ways.

Why the flowering of Armenian film? It is said that although the state kept its thumb over most of what was produced in the Soviet era, the state-run studio Hayfilm did not emphasize classical training in film as it did in painting or music. Therefore, filmmakers have not been tied to any particular traditions, and have been quite free to produce works that are truly their own expression.

The film industry takes center stage during the summer's Golden Apricot International Film Festival in Yerevan. Begun in 2004, the event seeks to build bridges across cultures and ethnic

groups. For example, it is not unusual for the festival to arrange a workshop led by both Turkish and Armenian filmmakers. Throughout the festival, Yerevan also puts on its best face with outdoor concerts and other exhibitions.

Where can one see Armenian film during the rest of the year? The locals flock to film screenings at the National Gallery of Armenia. Sometimes there are thematic screenings, but the most fascinating are those that offer question and answer sessions with film directors.

Music

As for music, at first glance it appears that the Armenian musical community is content to stick to the classics. The Opera House, for example, offers the Armenian State Philharmonic Orchestra performing chamber music, and whenever possible Armenian artists and productions are featured. Often, you can hear a performance of the music of the great Armenian composer Aram Khachaturian (a statue of him with his majestic hands is outside the opera building). Classical music can also be heard at several smaller venues, including the Yerevan State Musical Conservatory and the Chamber Orchestra Hall.

Otherwise, there is a clear preference for Armenian folk music, which is very different from

what one would hear in Eastern European or other
former Soviet Union countries. Traditional
Armenian folk music is based on a system of
tetrachords (not like the European octave), similar
to music of the Middle East or India. The last note
of one tetrachord in much Armenian folk music
also serves as the first note of the next tetrachord,
which theoretically makes the scale endless.

Armenia has developed its own instruments to
play its unique music. These include the *tar* (a
short-necked lute), the *duduk* (a reed
instrument), the *oud* (lute), and the *dhol* (drum).
You can purchase any of these instruments in the
Vernissage, although they are a lot more difficult
to play than they first appear. To hear great *duduk*
music you can pick up an inexpensive compact
disk of one of the masters at the Vernissage.

Folk dancing has also seen a revival. Children
learn these dances at an early age and get to practice
them at family events and weddings. Even in
restaurants or at parties, it is not unusual to see

groups of women stepping out into traditional routines on the dance floor. Most popular is the Armenian line dance, which can be simple or elaborate. It is quite possible for a Westerner to "fake" these moves without being too conspicuous. Be careful, though—a single Armenian folk dance can go on for fifteen minutes or longer.

Modern music tends to veer toward American and Russian pop and rock (music videos from both countries are prevalent at nightclubs, hotel gyms, and even hair salons). A few pop stars from Armenia are making headway, and there are many successful groups from the Diaspora (System of a Down, for example). There is also some interesting music on the jazz and avant-garde scene. The best known, the Armenian Navy Band, whose very name is a wry salute to their landlocked country, often performs in Yerevan.

Visual Arts

The visual arts were perhaps the most restricted arts during Soviet times. Directly after the fall of the Soviets, movements such as Cubism and the revolutionary styles of Kandinsky and Rodchenko were rediscovered. Unfortunately, there was also a period during the early 1990s when "anything that sells" was the order of the day. Since the economy has started to recover, however, artists have clearly felt a sense of liberation, and their new-found freedom is apparent in much of their work. Well-known contemporary artists include Karen Aghamyan, Arthur Sarkissian, and Hakob Hakobyan.

The work of experimental young artists can be seen in galleries and other venues across the Yerevan. Still, some artists prefer to stay away from galleries where owners often ask for exclusive or otherwise constricting contracts. These individuals prefer to display their work in the "free market" of the Vernissage, where artists sell directly to customers. True, the Vernissage painters include many traditionalists, offering paintings of Armenian dancers and lots of Ararat;

but look around and you will find many outstanding artists. Bright colors and somewhat abstract shapes are favorites of Vernissage artists. Another area where artists frequently display their work is the square by the Opera House.

Drama

The theaters put on plenty of traditional Armenian drama (the plays of William Saroyan are frequently performed). For avant-garde offerings, check what

is currently on at the Armenian Center for Contemporary Experimental Art, where artists act on just one square meter of stage, and perform other interesting exploits. Nearly all of these plays are performed in Armenian.

Other Entertainment

If you grow tired of theaters, art galleries, films, and concerts, or your children are begging for something a little more accessible, there are always the Dancing Fountains of Republic Square. The large public fountain is illuminated with colored lights and lasers, and the water "dances" to both classics and kitsch pop songs. On a warm summer night, it's good family entertainment, as well as a great opportunity to "people-watch" in downtown Yerevan.

For the most comprehensive updated list of cultural events, go to visitarm.com. The list of events is updated weekly and you can also have alerts sent to your e-mail. Also try to sign up for a Facebook group of Armenian artists. You will receive regular notices of where the next avant-garde production is being performed.

SPORTS

Not exactly a sport, but certainly a national pastime, is the game of chess. Armenia has won the biennial international Chess Olympiad in both 2006 and 2008. Chess tournaments are commonplace in Armenia's schools. And although you will see plenty of ardent backgammon players on the streets of Yerevan, the most intense competitors are those playing chess.

Soccer is popular, although in recent years the Armenian team's performance has not endeared it to its fans. Most soccer enthusiasts have a favorite European club, such as Real Madrid or Manchester United. EuroCup and World Cup are big events in Yerevan, where cafés air the games on large screens, to the delight of wagering fans.

Individual sports such as weightlifting, wrestling, and boxing are also popular. World champion boxer Vakhtang (Vic) Darchinyan, who was born in Vanadzor, Armenia, now lives abroad; but he remains a local hero.

chapter seven

TRAVEL, HEALTH, & SAFETY

Going to Armenia is an adventure. Because it is off the beaten track, you may need to do a little more preparation, but there will be rewards. While millions of tourists have seen the Eiffel Tower, how many have witnessed the majestic peak of Ararat on a clear, crisp morning?

Armenians are well prepared to welcome visitors, whether they are curious travelers or long-lost Diaspora cousins. There are many Web sites designed to highlight the places of interest within the country, and tourist agencies located in Yerevan and throughout the Caucasus region can put together guided tours and trips, as well as taking care of your accommodation in hotels or apartments. Some combine visits to Tbilisi with Yerevan.

Tours aside, it is quite possible to venture to Armenia without joining a formal group. Although knowledge of Armenian or Russian is certainly helpful, there are enough English-language speakers in Yerevan to assist where necessary, and there are plenty of restaurants and hotels where you will find food and relaxation. Just be prepared for some new experiences, and keep an open mind.

Young people with an Armenian heritage (at least one Armenian grandparent) who are between the ages of twenty and thirty-two may consider applying for a travel fellowship from the Birthright Armenia program. Those who are accepted are given free flights, placement with host families, get-togethers, and excursions, and in return give at least eight weeks of volunteer service in the country (usually outside Yerevan). They are expected to have a basic knowledge of the Armenian language, and instruction in this is made available to them if necessary.

VISAS

To enter the country, you will need a passport and a visa. Visas are required of all foreign nationals except those from the Commonwealth of Independent States and are relatively easy to obtain. You can purchase one at an Armenian embassy anywhere in the world, or even when you arrive at Yerevan's Zvartnots Airport. An entry visa is approximately $50, is valid for 120 days, and provides a one-time pass (if you leave the country it must be renewed—and paid for— upon reentry). It is also possible to get a one-year, multi-entry visa, which is considerably more expensive.

Foreign nationals wanting to stay more than 120 days for business purposes will need a letter from the company sending them to Armenia. The letter should describe the nature of the business performed, the name and address of a referee in Armenia, and a guarantee that your expenses are covered, as well as your return home.

Some foreigners may be eligible for ten-year Special Residency Status. Typically, this is given to foreign citizens of Armenian ancestry and those who have provided significant services to Armenia and are engaged in economic and cultural activities within the country. While in Armenia they enjoy the full protection of the Armenian law, and have the rights and obligations of Armenian citizens, except for the right to vote and to run for office. They are also exempt from military service. Survivors of the Armenian genocide used to also be provided this status without a fee.

When you leave the country there is an exit fee. Be sure to check what the current fee is (it tends to change) and leave yourself enough drams. You are required to have paid the exit fee before checking in for your flight.

ARRIVING IN ARMENIA

Your first encounter with Armenia will probably be at Zvartnots International Airport, outside Yerevan. Many flights into and out of Armenia are scheduled to arrive late at night or early in the morning, but don't worry. The airport will be in full operation to look after you.

Zvartnots is a source of pride for most Armenians. It was built in 1961, and opened its renovated arrivals terminal in 2006. The interior is bright, modern, and welcoming. You pass through shops, with young and eager sellers of duty-free wares, before going through customs. The customs officials are usually efficient, but you will have to

purchase your entry visa if you have not done so beforehand, and this may take some time.

From the airport there are buses and minibuses to take you into Yerevan (about 7.5 miles, or 12 km), or it's easy to get a taxi. In fact, there'll be a crowd of taxi drivers begging to drive you into town. Be forewarned, though, and look for a marked taxi, since unmarked cabs may greatly overcharge you. The journey should cost you about 4,000 to 5,000 dram, to which you should add a tip of 10 to15 percent). It is a good idea to agree on a price with the driver before getting into the cab.

GETTING AROUND IN YEREVAN

Once you are settled in Yerevan, you will find that—if weather permits—walking is the best option for normal movement around town, and is what most people do. If you prefer tracks or wheels, or if you're traveling some distance, there are subways, buses, taxis, and trains.

Yerevan is a relatively small city, and it isn't hard to walk the entire breadth of the central area in a couple of hours. But you should be aware that crossing the street can be treacherous. Also, the city is on a hillside and approximately 3,200 feet (975 m) above sea level. Although the hilly terrain is terrific for developing well-toned calf muscles, you may find yourself getting winded because of the high elevation. Breathing difficulties are especially common in the summer, when air quality is not always good. If you do get winded, find a park and a bench, and some Grand Candy ice cream—you deserve a break!

Crossing the Street in Yerevan
It is said that Yerevan is an extremely safe city, except when it comes to crossing the street. Pedestrians face serious risks when attempting to do so, and there have been bad and even fatal accidents.

Unfortunately, the phasing of traffic lights is not always reliable. Although the green "walk" signs may flash, cars still make fast turns through the intersection because the turn signals are not synchronized to allow for safe pedestrian passage. To add to the shock of nearly being run over, pedestrians crossing when the signal appears to be in their favor are sometimes treated to honking and fist shaking by drivers who believe they have the right of way.

When crossing busy streets such as Mashtots and Sayat Nova, cross at the green light and stop on the small painted island in the middle of the street. Wait there and make sure that even if the crossing light is green, there are no 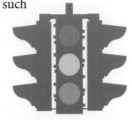 oncoming cars. Although it is tempting just to follow the locals as they negotiate the intersections, a second of hesitation may find you against the bumper of an aggressive vehicle. Always keep your eyes open and look in all directions before attempting to cross the street.

The Subway

The Yerevan subway is a very simple system consisting of just one line and ten stops. Built by the Soviets, it is old but efficient, and largely government subsidized. One ride costs 50 drams. Plans to expand the system were mothballed during the economic crisis of the 1990s, and have not been seriously reconsidered since.

How Yerevan Got Its Subway

Because of the city's steep hills, Yerevan residents and government officials wanted a subway system like other large cities in the Soviet Union. Yet, in the 1970s, the Soviet City Engineering Planning Department clearly stated that a subway system would be constructed only in cities with a population of more than one million. Nevertheless, the Armenians started digging tunnels—which they declared were for a streetcar line—against the time the population would be high enough to qualify.

By 1978 the underground infrastructure was completed, but the population requirement had not been met. The Chairman of the Armenian Communist Party, Karen Demirchyan, skillfully persuaded the Soviet Premier Leonid Brezhnev to disregard the rule. He reasoned that, "Each Armenian who lives away from his or her parents must visit them daily. As a result the passenger flow will be at least 1.5 times greater than projected. Moreover . . . sooner or later many of the Armenian Diaspora will want to return home." Demirchyan was so convincing that he got his subway.

Yerevan finally achieved a population of just over a million in 2006.

Marshrutkas (Shared Cabs)

If you find that the subway doesn't have a stop near your intended destination, one of the cheapest and most efficient ways to get around the country, in or out of Yerevan, is by shared

vans called *marshrutkas*. A ride in one of these costs 100 dram, and can take you almost anywhere along set routes. They can be crowded at rush hour, and you may find yourself a little too close to your companions, but it's reliable transportation.

Usually seating six to ten people, *marshrutkas* pick up and drop off passengers at *kangars* (bus stops), but outside the city center they will usually stop anywhere along their route if you signal that you want to get out.

The route numbers and landmarks or roads along the way are displayed in the windows (in Armenian). Watch for the route numbers, as these are really all you can see as they dash along the streets.

The *marshrutka* system follows a "hub and spoke" plan, with the larger towns providing local transportation to the surrounding villages, as well as to Yerevan. It is also possible to take one to Georgia or Karabagh.

Taxis

Taxis are relatively inexpensive in the city. There are official taxi stops, including the large gathering of

taxis at Sakharov Square, but you can flag one
down in central Yerevan at almost any time of day.
Most taxi drivers speak Russian in addition to
Armenian, and a few speak English, although this
is not common. Tipping the driver (10–15 percent)
is appreciated. Be careful with taking unmarked
taxis, as these tend not to have meters.

If you want to take a taxi for a long trip, such as
to Lake Sevan, or the Georgian border, it's wise to
arrange it in advance.

Rail

The railway system was recently taken over by
a Russian company. Trains in Armenia have a
reputation for being slow and not particularly
comfortable or convenient. The Yerevan Central
Train Station is located above the Sasuntsi Davit
subway stop. From here, you can catch a train to
Yumri, Lake Sevan, and Georgia. There are also
marshrutkas available for trips to Georgia and the
countryside.

Cars and Bicycles

Armenia is such a small country that driving
around should be quite simple. However, as
most foreigners soon discover, there are some
challenges, including finding your way around
poorly marked streets.

If you choose to drive in Yerevan, you are
braver than most foreign visitors. Those cars
that speed up to pedestrians are equally cavalier
with other drivers, and speed limits are often
disregarded. The police do issue tickets, but of
course they are not always around. Also, driving

along the center of a road's white line demarcations is considered acceptable. In the countryside, potholes and errant animals abound. Few cars are insured, and minor collisions and fender benders are quite common. Nevertheless, if you still want to drive, there are many car rental companies in Yerevan. They will rent you a car and wish you lots of luck as you take off!

Given the traffic situation, bicycling is relatively rare in Yerevan. Although bicycles are sold in Yerevan, they are mostly for children to ride in parks. Adult cyclists tend to be an oddity, so city drivers are surprised to see them and often disregard the courtesies usual in other countries. Bicycling in the countryside is a safer prospect if you're ready to tackle the hills. Most countryside cyclists prefer to travel in groups.

Finding Your Way

The good news is that finding your way around the major monuments and thoroughfares in Yerevan is relatively easy. The city still follows the plan laid out in the 1920s by Alexander Tamanian, whose contemplative statue greets visitors to the Cascade.

Although Tamanian envisioned a city of just a few hundred thousand residents, he laid out an ingenious circular series of broad avenues, key ring roads, and numerous shady parks. There are three major points of interest—Republic Square, the Cascade staircase, and, the true center of the city, the Opera House. The major streets (Mashtots, Bagrahmian, and Sayat Nova) all intersect at the Opera House. Even the new North Avenue leads to this central point in the city.

The bad news is that street signs and street addresses are not always prominently displayed. Also, important offices and residences are often in back alleys and side streets. The best thing is to ask for specific directions before venturing out to find a house or office. If you haven't done so, most taxi drivers can find the address you want either through

experience or by calling around to get directions. Simply hand the driver a piece of paper with your destination written down (preferably in Armenian). Also, Yerevan residents know that locating some out-of-the-way places can be frustrating for travelers, and are usually very helpful in giving directions. In fact, if you are standing in the street looking at a map, you are sure to be approached by people offering to help you. If they don't know the way, they will probably find someone who does.

DESTINATIONS

If you decide to travel outside Yerevan, your journeys should not be difficult. There are roads to take you to every major city or town, and if you are so inclined you could traverse most of the country within a week.

Outside Yerevan are the provinces, or *marz*, each of which has its own history and flavor. Because of all the monasteries in Armenia, some visitors make the mistake of assuming that this is all there is to see outside the cities. But there is much more.

Aragatsotn, in the west, is home to the Soviet-built Byarakan, one of the world's biggest astronomic telescopes, which offers amazing views of the heavens.

Armavir is located in the south, and is best known for the city of Echmiadzin, the center of the Armenian Apostolic Holy Church, and its cathedral, the oldest church in the world, built between 301 and 303.

Ararat was once one of the capital cities of ancient Armenia. It is the *marz* closest to Mount Ararat, and visitors can get a great view of the holy mountain from the Khor Virap Monastery.

Gegharkunik is where you'll find Lake Sevan, the largest lake in Armenia. Sevan is famous for its fish, but even more famous as a summer vacation spot for Yerevan's hot and bothered residents who come here to relax and barbecue.

Kotayk, to the north of Yerevan, will be a familiar name to beer lovers, as it is also borne by its famous liquid refreshment. This region is also home to the winter ski resort of Armenia's wealthier residents, Tsakhkadzor. Garni, the

ancient Greek temple, is located in Kotayk, as is Geghard, a picturesque monastery of the twelfth and thirteenth centuries.

Lori, which stretches across the northern border, is the largest *marz* and home to Vanadzor, Armenia's third-largest city. People in poor health come to Haghpat Monastery for its curative holy waters.

Shirak has as its capital Gyumri (formerly Leninakan), Armenia's second-largest city. Known as the "city of trades and arts," it is also famous for its schools and theaters. Armenia's first operatic performance took place in Gyumri in 1912, and the first Armenian opera house was opened here in 1923. This area was greatly affected by the 1988 earthquake.

Syunik is the southernmost *marz* of Armenia. It borders the Nakhchivan Republic to the west, Karabakh to the east, and Iran to the south. Its best-known city is Goris. Syunik is a green and mountainous area, but it is controversial in that it is also an area of intensive mining. Uranium mining by Russian companies in the village of Lernadzor has been a major topic of concern among environmentalists and local residents.

Tavush is in the northeast of the country, bordering Georgia to the north and Azerbaijan to the east. It surrounds the Barkhudarli and Yukhari Askipara exclaves of Azerbaijan, which have been controlled by Armenia since their capture during the Nagorno-Karabakh War.

Vayots Dzor, in the south of the country, is a very scenic *marz,* famous for the Noravank Monastery, considered the pulpit of the Syunik bishops. The resort of Jermuk, known for its mineral waters, is also here.

Artsakh (Karabakh) is a lush and rustic area, and a favorite of backpackers, but whether or not to go to the disputed region of Karabakh is a decision for you. If you do choose to go there you are limited to traveling by car or bus, as there is no airport or railway.

Wheelchair Access

Yerevan is making many improvements in increasing access for wheelchairs, and several buildings already have good facilities, though there remain many older buildings that have long staircases without ramps. Much of the advocacy for Armenia's disabled population comes from nonprofit groups which have exerted pressure on the government for mandating more widespread awareness. However, there are still places in the city where access can be a big challenge.

Taxi and minibus drivers will readily help those in wheelchairs, with little or no prompting, and

ordinary citizens will also usually lend a hand.
Don't be afraid to ask for assistance if you need it.

CURRENCY

The Armenian currency is the dram, which
currently (2009) stands at about 370 per
American dollar and 600 per British pound. After
Independence, the Central Bank of Armenia set its
value, but in 2009 the exchange rate was allowed
to float and the dram was greatly devalued.

The roller-coaster ride of the dram dates back
to the early 1990s. After the fall of the Soviet
Union, the Armenian economy was largely
dependent on US Diaspora dollars. In the early
2000s, the country was so flooded with US
currency that the dollar dramatically sank against

the dram (some say the
oligarchs brought about
this change in order to
import cheaper goods). In
2003, the Central Bank of
Armenia issued a decree
that dollars would no
longer be used as
currency, and mandated use
of the dram. Since than, the Central Bank has
been heavily promoting the dram, and even
erected a statue to it in Yerevan. With a 45 percent
increase in value over five years alone, the dram
was rumored to be in danger of succumbing to
unchecked growth, ultimately affecting local
producers, who would find it extremely
unprofitable to export their goods. On the other

hand, this growth was intended to benefit the few importers who wanted to continue procuring goods for lower prices.

With the recent devaluation the situation again seems to have changed. One thing is certain is that Armenia is currently a cash society. Although some supermarkets will take credit cards, almost all transactions are preferred in cash, in denominations of less than 20,000 dram (some markets will refuse to cash your 20,000 dram note). Checks and money orders are rare. Traveler's checks are accepted in some banks, but not by many merchants, and you are best advised to leave them at home, since you will become frustrated trying to use them. There are ATMs that dispense cash on almost every street in Yerevan. Most ATM screens have an "English" option.

Yerevan has several local banks and a few credit unions. Also, Armenia's banking legislation is among the most liberal in the former Soviet Union countries and there are no restrictions on foreign banks. Therefore, British and Western European banks are prevalent in Yerevan. HSBC has a large presence in the city, and staff members all speak English. Most banks, foreign and local, have English-speaking personnel.

Since many merchants request passports before making a large sale, it is wise to keep yours with you. Banks also require a passport if you want to make a significant withdrawal, and even the post office requests this form of identity when you are picking up a parcel. Driver's licenses are generally not accepted as proper identification, and many Armenians carry their passport with them at all times. There are few incidences of passport theft.

WHERE TO STAY

Today's traveler has several options for comfortable accommodation in Yerevan. Prices range from the very expensive to the extremely reasonable.

At the top of the list is the Marriott Hotel. Built fifty years ago in Republic Square (then Lenin Square), it was originally called the Hotel Armenia, and became widely known as the preferred establishment for foreign tourists in Yerevan. Having undergone a $38 million renovation in 2004, the Marriott is a resplendent example of architecture using Armenian tuf (the pink stone of Yerevan). Today, this five-star hotel in the center of the city is the largest American investment in the country and is also the "hub" for the English-speaking populace. On warm days, you can find many American and British citizens sitting at the Marriott's "Meeting Point" outdoor café, enjoying everything from hamburgers to quesadillas.

Compared to the Marriott, the Congress provides Western comforts at more reasonable prices. There is also an Italian restaurant on the premises.

For a little more Eastern atmosphere there are the Ani Plaza and the Golden Tulip, both of which have remnants of their Soviet past. The Ani Plaza is a pleasant establishment with smaller, functional rooms, but is not a "nonsmoking" establishment.

Smaller, less expensive hotels are available in Yerevan. They tend to be clean and functional. Check that there will be running water when you need it, especially in the summer, when several regions of Yerevan tend to have cuts in supply. Some hotels do not have elevators, in which case you must be prepared to carry your luggage up, possibly, several flights of stairs.

Be wary of hotels with casinos, especially those on the road to the airport. These are rumored to be affiliated with unsavory types, and generally do not provide foreigners with the type of service they expect.

Outside Yerevan

Outside Yerevan the most common places to stay are guesthouses owned by local families. Breakfast is included in the price. Although the accommodation may not be the most luxurious, these guesthouses offer an excellent opportunity to meet local residents and learn about life in rural Armenia.

You are also likely to find newer hotels in resort areas such as Tsakhkadzor. There are plenty of establishments for the superrich, housing conference halls, billiards and bowling facilities, disco bars, and spas—all, of course, for a significant price tag.

HEALTH

Armenia has socialized medicine, although the quality of services is sometimes lacking. The economic turmoil of the 1990s greatly strained the health care system, and the repercussions are still being felt, particularly in the rural areas. If you find yourself in need of a physician, contact your embassy, which should be able to provide you with a list of doctors who speak your language (many doctors speak English in Yerevan) and recommended hospitals for foreigners.

Armenian dental services are known to have high standards and offer treatment for a fraction of the cost of such services in America. Some Diasporan Armenians fly into the country specially to get high-quality dentistry done for the very reasonable price-tag.

SAFETY

Yerevan is known for being a safe city. Apart from the occasional older person asking for a handout, you are not likely to be approached by any shady characters. Most crime is relegated to auto theft and break-ins, and tourists are rarely targeted. It is also one of the few cities where women can confidently walk alone in the main areas at night.

That said, it makes sense to take some precautions. Women should avoid the deserted streets at night, and choose the backseat of the taxicab if traveling alone. Although the city runs on cash, be careful to keep your money secure, especially when carrying large denominations. Doors to hotel rooms and apartments should be locked upon leaving the building.

If you do find yourself the victim of a crime, you may go to the police, but most local police are more interested in activating their sirens and chasing traffic violators than tracking down thieves. You may find your attempt to file a report somewhat frustrating.

Armenia is earthquake country and appears to be relatively unprepared for "the big one." Few families keep earthquake supplies on hand. Cement buildings and crumbling stairwells abound, as well as parapets and other potentially lethal structures on the street. Another concern is the Soviet-era Armenia Nuclear Power Plant southwest of Yerevan. The plant was closed temporarily in 1988 following the devastating earthquake, but reopened in 1995. Armenia is currently under international pressure to close the plant permanently because of safety concerns.

Also be careful of wild dogs. These may appear friendly, and sometimes look cute enough for foreigners to want to adopt them, but these are feral animals and can be unpredictable. Additionally, many travel in packs. Stories of travelers being chased by packs of dogs are fairly common. It is best to respond to an approaching dog or dogs with the universal command, "Shoo!"

There is some risk of being caught up in Armenia's current political situation. As we have seen, in March 2008 a political demonstration turned extremely violent. At least ten people were killed as the government turned on the opposition. Foreigners should be mindful that even demonstrations intended to be peaceful could turn confrontational and possibly escalate into violence. You can tell when a demonstration is about to happen because police and soldiers will line up around the area. It's best to avoid it if possible, since tensions can run high.

chapter eight

BUSINESS BRIEFING

In the 1990s, all indications pointed to a miserable economic future for Armenia. The country was crushed by food and water shortages and limped along with just a few hours of electricity a day. It was crippled by the dissolution of the Soviet Union, pounded by the 1988 earthquake, and embroiled in a war with Azerbaijan. To most observers, there were virtually no hopeful prospects.

In the years that followed, however, Armenia experienced a growth in GDP of 10 percent per annum, and emerged as an economic leader in the

region. In the 2007 book *The Caucasian Tiger: Sustaining Economic Growth in Armenia*, the authors Saumya Mitra, Douglas Andrew, and Bartek Kaminski attribute this transformation to radical reforms, a commitment to keep inflation relatively low, and an influx of cash not experienced in many other post-Soviet countries. Because of these measures, the country came out of its despair and quickly became known as the best of the post-Soviet Caucasus countries for doing business. One World Bank report declared that Armenia has, "become a model transition economy that should continue prospering."

With all this good news, however, some provisos are necessary. Paramount is the understanding that the Caucasus area is known for its instability, so being best in the Caucasus still leaves room for improvement. For example, the Armenian workforce is still somewhat unstable because many job seekers may eventually seek employment outside the country. Based on recent surveys, approximately 100,000 people a year (3 percent of the population) emigrate to find work. Corruption remains a major concern, and closed borders continue to make trade difficult. In the words of the business journalist S. Adam Cardais, "[Necessary reforms] will take a lot longer than turning on the power."

THE BUSINESS CULTURE

The Armenians' historic acumen for business and trade has seen a resurgence in recent years. Typical businesses include the small, family-run company; the entrepreneurial start-up; the Armenian branch of a multinational company; and the big organization run by oligarchs. To get a good sense of the Armenian business scene, contact the Armenian Marketing Association (www.armenianmarketing.com) and ask for the annual Armenia Export Catalog.

Also, a new generation of businesspeople is emerging in the country, and it is very likely that the old ways of doing things will rapidly change. Today's young businesspeople have been thoroughly exposed to Western business practices and the qualities that are considered important for success in the global marketplace, and sometimes find themselves struggling with the older, Soviet-schooled generation. As a young Armenian businessperson said, "I am young, and I have no problem considering myself ambitious." However, he explained, older businesspeople (who tend to be the ones still in charge) were schooled in the Soviet style of management and do not usually appreciate "ambitious" young people who seem to have a natural understanding of computers, wireless technology, and more efficient approaches to business. "It is a constant struggle between old and new ways," said the young man.

Local Contacts and Personal Relationships
So what do you do if you have a business idea that you believe will do well in Armenia? First and foremost, remember that Yerevan (where most of your business will be) is a very small place, in the sense that whom you know and who knows you are very important. If you are related to someone

with a certain level of influence in the Armenian business community you'll find doors open quickly, even if you are only the distant cousin of a friend of a friend in Yerevan.

Coming in with a new business idea and no business contacts is inadvisable. As a foreigner you may be looked at with some suspicion, especially if you have no Armenian business contacts, but your chances of success will improve dramatically if you can manage to establish such local contacts.

MEETINGS

If you want to arrange a meeting in Armenia, your first challenge is to get past the most formidable gatekeeper of all—the office administrator. Many businesspeople complain that this person is charged with making it as difficult as possible to facilitate a meeting with his or her boss. ("Their job is to create as few tasks as possible for their bosses," says one businessperson.) You will probably hear your request for a meeting elicit an "It's not possible" from the officer administrator —several times. Even an e-mail sent directly to the person concerned is usually intercepted by the administrator, who will often respond with a negative answer. The secret of getting beyond the administrator is to secure your contact's personal mobile number. This is a great coup, but an important step, and one that should be pursued at great length.

If you do manage to secure a meeting, know that Armenians now prefer to set up their business sessions in a similar way to how this is done in the West. You should have an agenda, which you may want to submit to the office administrator beforehand. Those attending will appreciate being prepared for the meeting, and they will also want to know if you are running the session in English. There is usually no problem with this, but it is polite to give the warning.

Only a few years ago you would probably have met just with the business owner. Today, you will probably be meeting a team. In addition to the director are the specialists who are present because of their knowledge about something directly related to the topic of the meeting. This inclusion of the specialist has made it much easier to do business because the owner does not have to know—or pretend to know—about every aspect of the business.

Meetings typically start on time, but if there is a delay you will have an apology from your contact. Shaking hands is appropriate, and you should give your business card to all present. A card printed in both Armenian and English is a good idea, and will be appreciated. When you are presented with someone else's card, acknowledge it, and, if you are unsure of how to pronounce the name, ask how to do so. Addressing individuals by their first name is usually acceptable.

PRESENTATIONS

Although PowerPoint and LCD projectors are becoming common in Armenia, don't automatically assume that the proper equipment will be available. Check in advance with the office administrator. Apple computers are rare in Armenia, so if you are using a Mac and will require any technical assistance, ask ahead of time if anyone in the office is familiar with this brand.

Once you start the meeting, don't be surprised if cell phones ring, because everyone depends on these. Be prepared, also, for an undercurrent of talk, even while you are addressing the group. This may be a participant translating to another. (It may, on the other hand, just be a conversation.) There are likely to be many comments from the most senior person present, but be warned, too, that everyone will want to have a say. ("All Armenians have a little Napoleon in them," says one businessperson.) This is especially true during a meeting. As a visitor, it is your obligation to listen and be polite. However, if you are asked a lot of questions and elicit ample commentary this is a sign that your meeting is going well.

NEGOTIATIONS

The time that it will take for your counterpart to make a decision will depend mainly upon the size of the organization and the person in charge. If you are dealing with a small business owner who wants to get things done, the decision may be made quickly. In a larger organization things may move more slowly. It's quite possible that the person you originally met with does not have the final say.

As to your discussions, some negotiating is usually expected. This is almost always done in person and not by e-mail: it's important to be able to talk face-to-face. Don't adopt an aggressive style. Stay friendly and, if you can, show off a bit by mentioning people you know and the importance of your network. Also, take a lesson from the merchants in the Vernissage: you can haggle, but don't expect that you will always get exactly what you want. Armenian businesspeople are quite ready to step away from the negotiation if the price is not right.

CONTRACTS AND FULFILLMENT

In Armenia, the written contract is very important. Unfortunately, the contract is likely to be in the Armenian language, so make sure you have a good translator on hand. Despite computers and scanning devices, many businesses maintain printed contracts that they keep in files. Expect to sign numerous copies of the contract once an agreement has been met. You are also expected to keep a printout of your contract—don't expect that it has been scanned and stored digitally. After a contract is signed, you may offer to take your new partner out for a celebratory drink or lunch, but this is not expected.

If you run into problems, face-to-face conversations are best. You may find that your first encounter in a business dispute is with a junior person who will try to diffuse things but cannot rectify the situation. You should insist, tactfully, on meeting with the person in charge.

If there is simply no agreement, commercial disputes may be settled either in state courts or through arbitration. Commercial or property-related disputes may be settled by institutional or ad hoc panels of experts such as chambers of commerce or bank associations.

A WORD ABOUT CORRUPTION

Corruption remains a significant obstacle to doing business in Armenia. Granted, the problem is recognized and a number of reforms have recently been introduced, including simplification of licensing procedures, civil service reform, a new criminal code, privatization in the energy sector, passage of anticorruption laws and regulations, and the establishment of an Anticorruption Council. However, the problem still exists on a large scale, so must have a mention here.

Petty corruption is the most prevalent form experienced. It is not unusual for a businessperson to be required to pay a "tax" more than once, or to fill out so many forms that eventually one is informed that there are "more expedient ways" to get things moving.

Far more serious are the state-connected oligarchs who monopolize major products and services. These are the individuals who manipulate the domestic  market, dictating prices and currency valuation. These practices promote protectionism, encourage the creation of big monopolies that hinder competition, and undermine the government's efforts to foster private sector growth.

Of course, not all businesses are run by oligarchs, and not all government officials are corrupt. As a businessperson in Armenia, however, you cannot afford to ignore the possibilities.

WOMEN IN BUSINESS

The role of women in business is also undergoing significant changes. Raised by mothers who worked side-by-side with men in Soviet-run businesses, young Armenian women take their jobs very seriously. However, unlike their mothers, they are seeing the glass ceiling slowly lifting, and there is potential for them to advance in the business world if they are willing to give good customer service, work overtime, and take on projects beyond their usual job responsibilities. Many of these women are extremely bright and very capable, and have the ability to go far in the business world. Said one observer, "The future of Armenia rests in the hands of highly intelligent twenty-six-year-old women."

WANT TO GET AHEAD IN BUSINESS? GO TO A TRADE SHOW!

In a country as small as Armenia, and in a business environment where personal relationships are very important, one of the favorite activities is the trade show. Businesspeople use these shows to display their wares, engage in meetings, and socialize with colleagues.

When you're at a trade show, be sure to spend time talking with prospective clients and other exhibitors. The contacts you make will be invaluable.

As in the West, the elaborateness of your display and the quality of your samples are always important. And remember, because Armenians like doing business with Armenians, not to be surprised if one of the first questions you are asked is who you are connected with in Armenia.

chapter nine

COMMUNICATING

THE ARMENIAN LANGUAGE

> *Language is the roadmap of a culture.*
> *It tells you where its people came from*
> *and where they are going.*
> Rita Mae Brown

The Armenian language is generally classified as an independent branch of the Indo-European language family, and differs from its neighbors in appearance and grammatical structure. Some scholars see a connection between it and the ancient Hurrian and Urartian languages of Anatolia. Whatever its origins, it is fair to say that

Armenian is a unique and sophisticated language that has been a source of cultural pride for the Armenian people.

The hero of the language is Mesrob Mashtots, the fifth-century scholar and monk, later elevated to sainthood, who invented the Armenian alphabet (previously,

Greek, Persian, and Syriac symbols had been used, none of which adequately represented the complex sounds). After he had conceived the original thirty-six characters, an unprecedented educational movement began in Armenia.

Students were recruited to learn the new letters, and then to teach them to others. Further groups of scholars were sent to other countries to study and retrieve copies of the works of non-Armenian authors that could be translated into Armenian. This began with religious writings, but grew to include books on mathematics, medicine,

science, and astronomy. Ultimately, this concentration on language and literature inspired a golden age for literature and the arts in Armenia.

The official language of the Republic of Armenia is Eastern Armenian, also spoken by Armenians in Iran. With the movement of Armenians to the West in the nineteenth century came another version of the language, known as Western Armenian. Based upon the Armenian dialect of Anatolia prior to the genocide, and now mostly spoken by the Diaspora, this version of the language differs in some pronunciation and even some letters. Surprisingly, however, the Armenian spoken in the homeland remains remarkably intact since the time of Mashtots, in both characteristics and grammatical structure.

Thanks to the nation's education system, almost all Armenians can read and write their native language. Diasporan Armenians often require their children to learn their mother tongue. However, for the foreigner unfamiliar with Armenian pronunciation the language can be very difficult to learn. Several letters sound very similar, and there are a few consonants that have no similarity to sounds in other languages.

SURVIVAL ARMENIAN

Even if you don't become fluent in Armenian, it's easy to pick up a few useful words and phrases:

Barev	Hello (informal)
Barev dzez	Hello (formal)
Inch ka chika?	What's up?
Vonts es?	How are you? (informal)
Vonts ek?	How are you? (formal)
Shat lav	Very well
Ts'tesutyun	Good-bye
Kh'ntrem	Please
Sh'norhakal em	Thank you (*merci* is also acceptable)
Kenats't!	Cheers!

THE PHYSICAL SIDE

Armenians tend to be very demonstrative toward their friends. Members of the same sex hug and often kiss as they greet with exclamations of *Jan!* They may also hold hands, sometimes in twos, often with extended links to three to four abreast on the sidewalk.

Groups of men and women can also be very talkative, on the streets or on public transportation. Don't be surprised if you hear peals of laughter from a group of young women or men when on a bus or subway.

Speaking of public transportation, it is considered good form for a man to give up his seat for a woman, particularly an older one. Offering your seat will get you a *merci* and a smile.

If people smile at each other on the street, it is probably because they know each other. Unsolicited smiling is seen as a bit insincere and very "American." Also, effusive congratulations on accomplishments at work or in the classroom is seen as a gratuitous American "atta boy" attitude that rewards people for not necessarily accomplishing very much. The same goes for the handing out of certificates and trophies, which are seen as silly and meaningless.

Children evoke a smile from almost anyone. Armenians adore and dote on them. If you have children, don't be surprised if they are patted on the head or given a piece of candy or even a little gift by perfect strangers. Parents of infants sometimes feel that Armenians often take liberties in asking to look at or even hold the baby. Others will offer to watch your toddler as you negotiate the narrow aisles of grocery stores, for example. This can be a little disconcerting for new parents, but it is generally completely well-intentioned.

THE MEDIA
Armenians are divided on the status of their freedoms, especially when it comes to the press.

Some agree with the assessment of Reporters Without Borders that progress in press freedom has improved. Others point to events such as the protests of March 1, 2008 (see Chapter 1) and say that the government has severely clamped down on press freedoms. Recently, there have been several troubling reports of attacks on journalists and bloggers.

Although ostensibly a free press exists, most of the TV channels (the preferred source for news) belong either to pro-governmental political figures or to businesses heavily associated with the ruling party. Newspapers are owned by various politicians who slant the content. Circulation is also limited.

The most nonpartisan news media comes from online sources. The site A1plus.am actually began as a television station until it was forced off the air because it aired content in opposition with the ruling party. Recently, it has become a sizeable online news outlet that updates news several times a day.

The success of A1plus.am also led the government to start its own Internet daily news site, tert.am, and in a nod to keeping content balanced, two major columnists from the opposition were invited to write daily on the site.

There are also the completely independent bloggers. Several outstanding journalists are now filing reports from Armenia through Global Voices.com and their own blogs. An Internet newspaper, Hetq.com, also provides open, honest news stories, sometimes at their personal peril: the editor of Hetq was recently attacked in Yerevan.

Yet, if the local press is somewhat limited, Armenians have relatively free access to news from outside their country. Most homes in Yerevan are equipped with satellite television that beams in news reports from Russia, the USA (CNN), and the UK (BBC). And, of course, all those satellite dishes you see throughout Armenia are also beaming down plenty of entertainment programs. As well as Armenian productions, locals watch entertainment programs in English and Russian.

Russian periodicals and newspapers are readily available at almost every newsstand. However, don't expect to pick up a copy of the *Financial Times* or *International Herald Tribune*—publications in English are difficult to obtain.

TELEPHONE

When making calls from a landline, the local telephone system is relatively simple to use. Landlines are provided by the company Beeline (which also provides DSL), and Armentel and VivaCell are popular cell phone carriers.

Although plenty of older adults still use landlines, younger Armenians live by their cell phones. It is common practice for people to pick up their ringing phones no matter where they are—in class, in a business meeting, on a bus. Waiters have even been known to stop taking orders to pick up an incoming call.

If you are traveling to Yerevan, purchase or rent a GSM unlocked cell phone (if traveling to other countries make sure the phone will work there). SIM cards are relatively inexpensive once you are in the country, and will save you money in roaming charges.

THE INTERNET

Armenia is high on high technology. Almost every street in Yerevan has a computer store or Internet provider. This enthusiasm should not come as any surprise. At one time, Armenia was the technological hub, or Silicon Valley, of the Soviet Union. Young people were—and continue to be—encouraged to study computer sciences in school and to pursue IT as a profession. The site SiliconArmenia.com provides information on IT opportunities in Armenia.

However, there are limits to Armenia's enthusiasm for all things high tech. Although one can certainly purchase a laptop in Yerevan, it does come at a price. The same is true of all types of audio and video equipment. It is readily available, although often economically out of reach of the typical Yerevan resident.

As for the Internet, most businesspeople in Yerevan are beginning to use it as their primary form of communication. Some goods and services can be purchased online (there is a grocery store that offers online ordering); however, most of this is still somewhat in the future.

Dial-up services are the most prevalent form of connection in Armenia. One can purchase wireless, but it is still very expensive and users are often charged "download" and "upload" fees as part of their contracts. There are several projects afoot to offer wireless to even small rural communities, but these are still in the planning stages. Currently, if you are in need of Internet service, the best connection may be DSL, which is far more reasonable in price than wireless.

Most businesses in Armenia are expected to have a Web site. Usually, this is a basic site with product and contact information. They are generally in English or Armenian, with a Russian translation available. E-commerce and Web 2.0 (highly interactive programs) are still relatively rare for Armenian businesses. Blogging is very popular with young people as a form of personal communication, especially through the platform Live Journal.

MAIL

The mail service is something that most Armenians would rather not talk about. Although several of the mail stations have been updated, Hay Post (the state postal service) remains an antiquated system. Getting a package sent from another country can be extremely slow and frustrating. It is not uncommon for a parcel to arrive one to two months after it was sent.

Although there is usually someone at Hay Post who speaks English, it is not guaranteed. Hay Post is also where people pay household bills, so you may have to stand in line for a while before you can mail a package or retrieve a long-lost one.

CONCLUSION

For those who live in cities with large Diasporan Armenian populations, it is easy to form a highly romanticized view of the country. Only in Armenia can one begin to understand the continuing struggle of the proud Armenians to preserve their beloved Hayastan. While other small countries have given way to conquering nations or allowed their customs and traditions to fade away, Armenians have always held out against the pressure to assimilate.

When you are there, be sure to talk to people of different generations. From the elders you will hear stories of life during Soviet times, stalemated wars, shortages, and a longing for their beloved Mount Ararat. From young people, you will learn their hopes for the future of their country. You will get to know and respect these proud realists who understand that they have a shared responsibility to preserve what has been fought for and passed down to them and to their own children.

Remember that a visit to Armenia is only worthwhile if you shed preconceived notions and open your heart and mind. Do not bristle at the way things are done in a land where everyday life tends to have its challenges. If you listen to the people, absorb the beauty of the country, and appreciate its long history, you will be inspired by this ancient land and its proud, warm, and tenacious people.

Further Reading

Akcam, Taner. *A Shameful Act: The Armenian Genocide and the Question of Turkish Responsibility*. New York, NY: Holt Paperbacks, 2007.

Avakian, Arra. *Armenia: A Journey Through History*. Fresno, CA: The Electric Press, 2008.

Balakian, Peter. *Black Dog of Fate*. New York, NY: Basic Books, 2009.

De Waal, Thomas. *Black Garden: Armenia and Azerbaijan Through Peace and War*. New York, NY: NYU Press, 2004.

Melkonian, Markar. *My Brother's Road: An American's Fateful Journey to Armenia*. London: I. B. Tauris, 2008.

Mitra, Saumya, Douglas Andrew, and Bartek Kaminski. *The Caucasian Tiger: Sustaining Economic Growth in Armenia*. Washington, DC: World Bank Publications, 2007.

Payaslian, Simon. *The History of Armenia*. New York, NY: Palgrave Macmillan, 2007.

Films

Egoyan, Atom (Director). *Ararat*. Miramax, 2002.

Goldberg, Andrew. *The Armenians: A Story of Survival*. Two Cats Productions, 2000.

Useful Resources

http://www.armeniabirding.info
Birds and the ecology of Armenia

http://www.armenianhistory.info
Extensive history of Armenia

http://armenianodar.blogspot.com/
Myrthe Korf's blog on life and books in Armenia

http://www.armeniapedia.org
Online encyclopedia [wiki]

http://www.armsite.com/
Armenian art and culture

http://hetq.am/en/
Reports from Armenia

http://www.hyeetch.nareg.com.au/republic/index.html
Online book about Armenia

http://oneworld.blogsome.com/
Reporter and photographer Onnik Krikorian's Armenian blog

Index

Acknowledgments

I am very grateful to the many Armenians and expatriates who helped me both in Yerevan and back in California. In particular, I wish to thank Nona Sark, Artak Aloyan, Myrthe Korf, Aram Navasardyan, Tigran Matosyan, Arminé Nalbandian, Arthur Khoyetsyan, Michael Nicholson, Leah Kohlenberg, Joseph Ribakoff, and Gayane Dallakyan.

Above all, this book is dedicated to my family, Joe, Sam, and Shira Ribakoff, with whom I was privileged to share our great Armenian adventure.